D0977007

HOLE
IN THE
SKY

HOLE
IN THE
SKY

A MEMOIR

WILLIAM KITTREDGE

ALFRED A. KNOPF

NEW YORK

1992

Copyright © 1992 by William Kittredge
All rights reserved under International and Pan-American Copy-
right Conventions. Published in the United States by Alfred A.
Knopf, Inc., New York, and simultaneously in Canada by
Random House of Canada Limited, Toronto. Distributed by
Random House, Inc., New York.

Portions of this book have appeared, in slightly different form,
in the following publications: *Esquire, Harper's, Hayden's Ferry
Review, Modern Maturity, Outside, Ploughshares,* and *Witness.*

ISBN 0-679-41166-6

LC 91-58670

Manufactured in the United States of America

Published June 10, 1992
Reprinted Once
Third Printing, October 1992

For

Gert and Al
Maude and Will
Jo and Oscar
Pat and Roberta
Karen and Brad
Zach, Riley
Max, and Leo

CONTENTS

Thanks to Carol and Ivan Doig, who got me centered on the idea of this book in the first place; to Amanda Urban, who saw me through all the changes; to Gary Fisketjon, whose fine pencil helped it so much; and to Annick Smith, whose help is, and always has been, of course, invaluable

HOLE
IN THE
SKY

CHAPTER 1

FALLING

Maybe children wake to a love affair every other morning or so; if given any chance, they seem to like the sight and smell and feel of things so much. Falling for the world could be a thing that happens to them all the time. I hope so, I hope it is purely commonplace. I'm trying to imagine that it is, that our childhood love of things is perfectly justifiable. Think of light and how far it falls, to us. To *fall*, we say, naming a fundamental way of going to the world—*falling*.

The year I was to turn six, the spring of 1938, out in the backlands of southeastern Oregon, I began a curious, end-of-innocence time, trying to fathom what there was to value about life. I was fresh from something like a year in hospital rooms, recovering from polio. People said I had almost died; I wanted to know why it was better to be alive.

At this moment I am nearing sixty, and wish I could go back to the world inside that child. I want to reinhabit his direct curiosity about himself, to know as that child knew. I want to smell the sour stink of springtime, and taste the air as I stood out on the lawn in front of the house my father had built for us.

The men who worked on our ranch were hauling manure from the corrals on horse-drawn stoneboat sleds, rebuilding the long dams across the swales in the hay meadows, flood-irrigating the swamp grasses, which had all at once turned brilliantly and variously green, sedges and field lilies, and tules in the sloughs. Waterbirds would come and go, and my father would worry about coyotes killing spring calves, and raccoons in the nests of ring-necked pheasants, sucking eggs in thickets of willow that were sprung to leaf. The world was beginning to accumulate an irresistible momentum.

Around May 10 the homesteader's row of Lombardy poplars in front of our house would crack their heart-shaped buds. The translucent lime-green leaves would emerge, and cast their tiny flittering shadows over my mother's face as she studied the morning. I thought the world was alive like a creature, and it was. Soon the lilac would blossom. It was the high beginning of true spring. My father's twenty-four-hour-a-day frenzy of farming was just about finished. On the far side of Warner Valley thousands of acres of flood-irrigated plowground had been disced and harrowed and drilled to oats. There was nothing left but to watch the growing, and hope the killing frosts were behind us.

In the evening my father would drive along the canal banks to study his crops as they emerged in undulating rows across the dark peat soil of the old swamplands. We would speculate on how much the seedlings had grown in just one day. We thought we could smell the growing. That little boy had no intimation that those moments would come to stand in memory as his approximation of perfection: his family, his life before him, the world in renewal.

Warner Valley is the main staging ground for my imagination. We never learned much in the way of local and family history, but I know my own stories, and Warner is a landscape where the names of people are connected to things that happened around me, and what happened reminds me of where, and then we are back to the landscape and another round of connection.

What I want to recall are mornings when I would go outside by myself, just after daybreak. I would slip from the bedroom I shared with my younger brother, while he was sleeping, and wander barefoot on the lawn still wet with dew. The air was thick with the reek of damp sage and greasewood and the raw odor of the apple orchard in full blossom, and the stench of cowshit from the shed where Clyde Bolton milked the three cows my father insisted on keeping. That boy felt like he was full of the world, breathing it into himself, and he was.

His thinking is easy to remember; I don't know why he had come to his thoughts but I recall how carefully he tried to think them through, and how he came to tell himself there was no reason for anything except for this pleasure in the love of what we are. I would like to reclaim the ease and clarity with which I was able to think about what I was and what I wanted.

That very young boy, out on the lawn under the new leaves of the poplar, beside the white house: the waterbirds in their great V-shaped flocks above him in the springtime sky. He can hear them calling, so many birds, hundreds of thousands of waterbirds. In those years, according to wildlife biologists, a quarter-million waterbirds moved through Warner every spring, going north to the Canadian and Alaskan and Siberian tundra, to the enormous rivermouth marshes where the Mackenzie and Yukon empty into the sea. That boy is trying to make an intellectual shape out of his feelings for the world. Those waterbirds, calling and honking, undulating against the sky like music we

used to know, birds beyond numbering. It is always pure pleasure to begin naming them: green-winged teal and blue-winged
teal and cinnamon teal and redheads and canvasbacks and buf-
fleheads and mallards and white-winged snow geese and the
Canada honkers and the lesser Canadians.

It's a list I've run through many times. Rilke says, in the
ninth Duino Elegy, *"Perhaps we are here in order to say: house, bridge,
fountain, gate, pitcher, fruit-tree, window"*— It was just that nobody
in my family could agree on anything, much less the right life.
At the end we had more than twenty-one thousand irrigated
acres in Warner Valley, something beyond another million acres
of leased Bureau of Land Management rangeland. We ran more
than six thousand mother cows. It could have been a paradise;
maybe it was, maybe it still is.

The Great Depression was hanging over most everybody in our
outback part of America, but my father was harvesting huge
grain crops, and it was being said that he had "turned things
around." People were beginning to look to him for help.

Some distant relatives came to talk about taking a job. I
remember their black, square-doored Model A pickup truck
loaded with their crated possessions, and there *she* was. I knew
her at once, in a quite classical recognition: little girl, maybe
five years old. It was simple and immaculate; drawn to her like
an animal sensing home, on a bright autumn day in our lost
valley amid the sagebrush distances, the sweep of our oncoming
lives feathering away before us, I was in what I recognized at
once as love.

Those people are not real to me. In my memory I can't see
their faces. I can only remember my excitement, and the way
my mother teased me about it, and the degree to which I was

furious and then utterly devastated when the little girl was taken away; her father didn't want the job after all. I was frantic as their Model A went down over the hill toward the headquarters ranch house, where they would spend the night. And then I ran away, headlong down that road in their dust. I followed them, and my father had to go after me. He was hugely amused, as I recall, trying to jolly me out of my misery as he drove me home, but I couldn't sleep for a long time, and then it was all fading like a dream when I woke up to sunlight the next morning.

It is a little surprising (maybe unbelievable) to remember that child who was myself, and his short inconsolable heartbreak. He lay in his bed that night and thought he hated his mother and his father and thought he understood how things could fail him in some religious way (not ever be enough), and how clearly he saw this as the beginning of emptiness. Then the world in its beguiling radiance came back to him in the sunlight of the next morning, and he felt shame because he couldn't recall that little girl very clearly. The child I was, he was trying to think. That is what I think I remember. I wonder if children have such thoughts.

I think of walking down the quarter mile to the ranch headquarters, and watching as the blacksmith pumped his bellows until the fire was white hot, and the times he let me pound and shape some glowing iron bar, then plunge it into the cold water for tempering. I learned the colors of heat, from white to cherry red, and loved knowing that there was so much to know.

I think of my own son, maybe twenty years later, at a picnic on Deep Creek the summer he was four. "I looked down," my wife said, "and there he was, under the water, looking up. He was smiling." The way she told it he wasn't frightened at all until he was out of the water and saw how frightened *she* was. Maybe this is a set of sad stories about the ways we learn to

distance ourselves, and teach our children such distance. Maybe
it is a cautionary tale. But I hope not. I want this to be a story
about the way a sense of connection to the energies of everything can sweep over us; and why I think that sense of connection is supremely valuable.

Through all this I am most concerned to examine the
possibility that I may come to die and feel myself slipping back
into everything. I hope I may feel that such slipping back into
things is proper while it is happening. I hope I will be happy in
the going, though sometimes that seems only like another way
of saying I'm frightened and furious. I want to be like the child
for whom it was so simple to let himself go into affection for
what we are. He loved it as we seem to in the beginning, on
the doorstep of life, with a future so thick in second chances.

What a release it might be, falling back into the world as if
through some gate that was reopened, into that time in which
we felt ourselves seamlessly wedded to every thing, and every
other thing, getting closer.

I want to see if the light is really burning. I want to see the
Lombardy poplars and apple trees and the posts supporting the
woven-wire fence around the house where I lived in that boyhood, I want to see if they are glowing in the luminous world.
I want *things* to be radiant and permeable. I want to be welcome
inside these memories if nowhere else, and think I was welcome
when I was a child. I want the child who thought about the
world and understood that he was welcome to have been correct. I want to have had that; I want the world to be that good.

We yearn to escape the demons of our subjectivity. We yearn
to escape our selves, into intimacy. We yearn to sense that we
are in absolute touch with things; and we are, of course.

There is in all of us an ache to care for the world. So why do we seem to have such trouble connecting to one another in even the most simple-minded, hand-holding ways? We don't seem able to understand what is generosity and what is selfishness, and in consequence we educate ourselves into two-hearted confusion as we try to define our responsibilities.

We want to know: where are we, and why were we ever born? We want to understand why we need to understand. Something is wrong, part of us is missing, we know it. Do we just dissolve, like light in the evening sky?

We are very frightened: we are driven to the unending and utterly impossible task of trying to heal ourselves back into whatever it is we understand as holy. We dream of childhood, sex and music and the beauty we can see. We find religion.

People go walking into nature. They say they feel they are becoming part of things. They say they want to be like a stone, or a flower; they say such release from the self is bliss, a kind of religious ecstasy, and they want it over and over.

But you have to wonder. Philosophers argue that we cannot be aware of ourselves without language. They say we are created by our language, that we live immersed in language and cannot escape; they say language stands as a scrim between us and what we think of as "real," and that we have to name things before we can know them. As a result we can never know what is "actual." All we can know is names, stories.

Those are the arguments. Maybe the people who go for walks are not connecting with anything at all, and find their joy simply by slipping out of the world for a while and refusing to participate. Perhaps that's all I'm looking for as I seek to reinhabit the child I imagine as myself: a way out, like a drug.

I hope not. What I am looking for, at least so I tell myself, is a set of stories to inhabit, all I can know, a place to care about.

Up the Skeena River in the cloud-park interior of British Columbia, across the road from the Tsimshian village of Kitwancool and framed by a stand of aspen beside the creek, there is a cluster of cedar totem poles from the early days. Carvers are considered high artists among the Tsimshians, and there are nineteenth-century poles at Kitwancool which bear comparison to the most vivid work of Matisse or Picasso, at least in the clear way they remind us of our true situation.

Among them is the house pole called Hole in the Sky. An oval hole cut through the base of the house pole serves as a ceremonial doorway into the long cedar-plank building where the families lived. The hole in this particular pole, as I understand it, was also thought of as "a doorway to heaven," in the literal sense.

The Tsimshians believed that stepping into your house was stepping into a place actually populated by your people, all of them, alive or not—the dead at least to the extent that they were remembered by anyone. It is a lovely notion, the space inside the house connecting to the landscape of communal imagination, the actual place bound together with story and recollection. It is like what I understand as the Latin sense of *familia*, meaning both house and family: a sandbar along Deep Creek, and willows, the humming pulse of a midsummer day, and my son looking at the sun through a lens of clear water.

But there is, of course, another kind of hole in the sky, which is the simple emptiness we may take as a modernist idea of God. We all know it in our way.

A long look in that direction, on the unforgettable morning of April 11, 1961, frightened me almost unto death, and drove me through some frantic years of trying to name what was real, and figure out which story was mine, which was family, and which politics. I shook with terror in my bed at night, and understood that I was utterly alone; I couldn't get myself to believe that I was enclosed in anything like a run of specific glories, that I breathed them, that in some sense they were me. That dis-ease took decades to cure, if it is cured.

This is meant to be a book that is useful, about the stories I learned to tell myself in my most grievous isolations. Most of all it is supposed to be a book about taking care inside whichever dream we inhabit.

CHAPTER 2

TERRITORY

In 1660 Captain John Kittredge fled from England to America. Captain Kittredge was in charge of a ship which plied from England to some foreign port. He had in charge, medical receipts, and being of a surgical turn of mind, he studied them carefully. He began experimenting by breaking an animal's limb; then setting them, seeing how fast he could get them to heal. One of his men broke an arm, and the Captain set it. Soon after this, another man broke a leg, and asked the Captain to set it for him. The Captain said he would, "if he would take a room and place himself entirely in his care"; to which he did. He being very successful, it became known to the authorities, and as the laws were very stringent at that time, allowing no one to practice without a medical diploma, it became necessary for him to flee from England, and come to this country, where he settled in Billerica, Mass., September 25, 1660.

—MABEL T. KITTREDGE,
The Kittredge Family in America

For many generations the major players in my family were centered in Massachusetts, but there are lost tribes, like ours, scattered everywhere. It has been a family that took pride in its doctors and teachers and occasional Harvard intellectuals (the best known being the great scholar of English literature, George Lyman Kittredge), but mine were most often agricultural people.

It is a story that has been documented with considerable in-house mania. Every so often I get a letter from some stranger who writes to tell me that we are related, occasionally enclosing genealogical charts to prove it. I used to think this impulse was sad and unseemly, that we should not be so driven to grasp at our connections to life. But I have changed my mind; I want to know what there is to know about my connections. Those people are trying to find themselves in a story which will make their lives meaningful and coherent. So am I.

In 1826 a Dr. William Kittredge took himself and his new bride west from Massachusetts to Michigan, where he practiced medicine in Ypsilanti and Grand Rapids. My great-grandfather, Benjamin Franklin Kittredge, was born in 1828, the oldest of eight children. In 1850, aged twenty-two, Benjamin Franklin took his younger brother Harrison and headed west for the goldfields of California. You have to wonder about the intensity that drove those boys, really not much more than children. Imagine the stories they were telling themselves.

Ben Franklin and Harrison were not poor boys. Their father was a doctor so they had to be leaving home for more than a chance at easy money.

For many travelers, we know, and not just young men with an itch, it was simply a desire to go *out*, away to the world with hope of discovering some interesting fate. Families sold good farms in Ohio and rolled west in their wagons, and often were destroyed before they were done, driven to ruin by what came down to nothing more profound than a yearning for excitement, a thing so simple as one chance at a life which was not boring, a happy land over the mountains.

Benjamin Franklin was a single man, and it is easy to imagine his leave-taking might have been simple. Good-bye to your sweetheart and father and mother, a kiss to the younger children, and you and your brother can just walk away. What will you be?

Benjamin Franklin and Harrison made their passage down the Mississippi and across the Gulf of Mexico to the narrows at Panama long before there was any canal, where they set off and just walked to the Pacific. And then another boat ride, this time to San Francisco. But gold didn't come easy. There was winter, snow and mud in the camps, and Harrison was killed in a dispute over a mining claim. There are no details, but I imagine some showdown over a shovel or a hundred yards of creekbed. Even if Harrison was justified in his anger, if that was the scenario, he was dead.

Ben Franklin went home. Back in Michigan, he married, and he came west again, this time in a wagon, with all the goods of his marriage, back to the gold camps, where he had no more luck than before. A first son, Herbert, was born in a camp known as Jackass Flats, outside Redding, California, on June 8, 1863. After some seasons in the foothills around Mount Shasta, panning little streams for trace, Benjamin Franklin moved his family north, always moving, as if to examine the promise of things. He owned acreages in the Willamette Valley of Oregon, some of the finest agricultural land in the world, but nothing came of it.

In 1875, my grandfather and namesake, William Kittredge, was born, the seventh child of nine, while Benjamin Franklin was a schoolteacher at old Fort Simco, near Yakima in Washington. Later the family moved south beyond the gorge of the Columbia River, to a ranch in the hillslope country near Antelope, Oregon (where the Bagwan Rashneesh set up his freeloading version of heaven in the mid-1970s), then to some fringes of mostly salt-grass meadowland in the far outback around Silver Lake, Oregon. And there his life ended in 1898, flat out of possibilities.

My grandfather was then twenty-three, and poor. I wish I knew what he thought as he lifted his eyes to study the scrubbrush flats around Silver Lake. I wish I knew how resolve came to him, and how he named it. I wish I knew what he saw as the gifts life might give him.

For a long time my grandfather was the most powerful figure in my life, and I learned to despise him. In May 1958 he fell from his chair at the pinochle table. I wish I could at least guess at what he thought as the light vanished. Life had given him great properties. What were they worth in the end? I wish I had talked to him before he died. I wish mine had been people who lived in a tradition of such talking.

The northern quarter of the Great Basin, southeastern Oregon and northern Nevada, is a drift of sagebrush country the size of France. The raw landforms incessantly confront us with both geologic time and our own fragility. The rims were built over eons; we can see the layers, lava-flow on lava-flow. Shadows of clouds travel like phantoms across the white playas of the alkaline wet-weather lakes. But the endlessness of desert is not so intimidating if you focus on the beauties at your feet, red and green lichen on the volcanic rocks, tiny flowers.

That landlocked country is not all desert, and there are

mountains where the snows accumulate. Along the northern edge of the Great Basin are Bidwell Mountain and the Warners, and the Ochocos, where the Silvies River gathers north of Burns. Fault-block upliftings rise from the distance like islands, the ten-thousand-foot escarpment of Steens Mountain, Hart Mountain and Winter Rim in Oregon, the faraway Ruby Mountains of Nevada.

The most significant geography, so far as settlement was concerned, lay below those mountains in the oasis waterfowl valleys. The snows melted and ran off in spring floods, land-locked lakes filled and dried and refilled, the sedges and tules grew and died and rotted away into peat soil. Those valleys formed wetland enclaves: Surprise Valley, Warner Valley, Blitzen Valley, Ruby Valley. Without them that country would have been free of white settlement much longer than it was.

In Warner we lived surrounded by immense distances, and yet we were safe in our refuge. The conjunction of wetland and desert seemed like a true condition of life; the valley stank of water and rot and fecundity and you could smell it from miles away, as you came horseback across the alkaline flats.

Before the white men came in the latter half of the nineteenth century, this country was populated by a scattering of northern Paiutes and traveling bands from the timbered country to the west, Klamaths and Modocs who came to the swamplands for the waterbird hunting.

The northern Paiutes believed a traveler could slip into caves under the rimrocks and find an underworld of creatures. Trout were thick in the streams; they would rise like ghosts to feed on grasshoppers in the aftermath of a thunderstorm. The green moss would be spongy and rich under your feet. The ripe berries would fall into your hands. The mule deer would look back at you without apprehension, ears twitching at the little flies. It was the place where the game animals lived before they emerged to share the world with us.

This was not altogether a fantasy; in fact it's a fairly precise description of what you can find today along the tiny streams which rise in the isolated Great Basin ranges, and flow down to the swamplands where the waterbirds congregate.

Stories of an underworld populated by that richness of animals were not likely dreams at all, in the beginning. But no one knows what those people thought, actually, or anything about their dreams. I don't think anybody I knew realized that some parts of the place where we lived had been so magical in the imaginations of another people.

The northern Paiutes seem to have been what we think of as a deeply primitive people, who did not have much in the way of what anthropologists call "cultural items," a list which includes everything from spoons to ideas of magic. They lived sparse and traveled light. The country did not reward them for owning things. The clan which lived around my home territory in Warner Valley was known as the Groundhog Eaters, a name wonderful in its inelegance. You wonder what it meant to them as they managed lives which no doubt did not seem either splendid or numbing or even simple.

Some of us like to imagine that those people understood that the world was alive, and their true companion. The idea that they had always lived in communality is not entirely sentimental. There are people who move through their cycles of hunting and gathering thinking everything is alive, regarding life as a series of ceremonies, measuring time by events like birth, initiation, marriage, children, and death.

Some of us like to suppose that the people we call native

live in quietude in a world in which they understand that everything is part of every other thing. Such lives are very difficult for us to imagine; it is even more difficult for most of us to value them. We are infected by an urge to go conquer time, to be individual, to write books, and break out new plowground. We know it, but don't think we can help it.

Some of us envy the existence of such people in their endless sway of time. Others despise that envy as softheaded and primitivistic. What we know for sure is simple, and brutal: such people are almost gone from the earth and within another couple of generations their dreams will be extinct.

In Warner Valley there is a long curl of high ground along the eastern side of Crump Lake, which is known locally as the Bar. Those people camped there in waterbird season, over millennia. Up until the early 1930s, the Bar was thick with wild roses and native berry brush. Then, in the devastating series of dry seasons which accompanied the economic ruination of the Great Depression, the tule-ground flood-plain around Crump Lake caught fire and the thickets of dry chest-high brush burned away, leaving reefs of ashes across a litter of beautiful chipped obsidian artifacts which had been lost, accumulating over centuries.

Think of afternoons on the Crump Lake Bar, amid the rose-bushes, the waterbirds clattering as they come and go. At that latitude and elevation there are days in the fall when the sunlight lies like glory over the dying red-orange reeds of the tule-beds and the muddy soft water. You could voyage into that faraway country and try sitting quiet alongside a seep spring deep in the hidden backlands, and study the singular beauty at the heart of a desert flower while long-legged insects walk the surface tension of the water. Your concern with the passage of time might ease, you might be inclined to attempt the slow day-to-day dance of creatures.

You might feel you had gone somewhat native, and you might be right. The native people were much like us; it's just that our people killed them like animals, gave them our diseases, and drove them to the arts of farming and rodeo. In Warner Valley we lived surrounded by ghosts, but we forgot.

That huge drift of country is pretty much nonexistent in the American imagination. The whole of it—Lake and Harney and Malheur counties in Oregon, Washoe and Humboldt counties in Nevada, each as large as some states in the East—is still populated by no more than a few thousand people.

Sensible routes of travel, wagon trails and railroads, went around to the north (the Oregon Trail) or to the south (the California Trail). Settlement by white men with families, who were intent on setting up ranches, did not begin until the 1870s. After the Mexican-American War, in 1848, drovers began trailing herds from Missouri to the central valley of California. One of the men who was in on those drives from the beginning was Dr. Hugh Glenn, a young Virginian whose ambitions influenced a considerable part of history in southeastern Oregon. Before a decade had passed, Dr. Glenn owned one of the enormous Spanish ranches in the Sacramento Valley.

In 1859 the miners around Virginia City in Nevada found that the black rock they had been discarding was silver, and the Comstock boom began. The miners didn't want much more than a place to dig; but they had to eat, and the people who fed them felt they had a right to run livestock anywhere that was handy, including the creek-side meadowlands where the Truckee River emptied into Pyramid Lake. The Indians traditionally camped there in early spring, coming for hundreds of miles to work the cutthroat trout fishery. Winter was over, there was food for all.

In 1859 two Paiute girls were kidnapped and abused by two brothers at Williams Station, a whiskey stop on the Carson River. A party of warriors killed the brothers and burned the station. Then began a series of battles across northern Nevada, initially called the Pyramid Lake War, which never really ended until the natives were effectively broken and driven to the reservations. Six years later, in March 1866, the *Humboldt Register* described a battle:

> At half past nine the order was given to charge. Right merrily the men obeyed. The Indians stood up bravely, fighting sullenly to the last—asking no quarter; but the charge was irresistible. The boys rode through the Indian ranks, scattering and shooting down everything that wore paint . . . eighty warriors, thirty-five squaws. The latter were dressed the same as the bucks, and were fighting—and had to be killed to ascertain their sex.

The U.S. Army was determined to subdue the natives and protect the settlers, and to establish forts and encampments as a foundation for governing the wilderness. In the best book on the subject of prewhite storytelling in Oregon, *Coyote Was Going There; Indian Literature of the Oregon Country*, Jarold Ramsey writes:

> The white response, organized during the Civil War, was brutally simple: extermination. The unpublished "Field Journals" of Lt. William McKay (a medical doctor who was himself part Indian) made it vividly clear that Army detachments like McKay's, aided by Indian scouts from Warm Springs and elsewhere, went through the upper reaches of the Great Basin country hunting Paiutes and other Shoshoneans down like deer, killing for

the sake of what in the Viet Nam era became known as "body-count."

By the summer of 1868 the Indians in northern Nevada and southeastern Oregon were being rounded onto desolate reservations. An educated Paiute woman named Sara Winnemucca, employed as a liaison for the army, found starving bands of her people collected at Camp C. F. Smith in far southeastern Oregon. She sent fifteen wagons for the children, and some eight hundred Paiutes were moved to the reserve at Fort McDermitt, on the Oregon-Nevada border, where they were issued daily rations. Sara Winnemucca helped hand out the food, and hated what she saw. She wrote to Major Henry Douglass, Indian superintendent of Nevada: "If this is the kind of civilization awaiting us on the Reserves, God grant that we may never be compelled to go on one, as it is much prefferrable [sic] to live in the mountains and drag out an existence in our native manner."

The open range was pretty much taken up in California. Stock growers who wanted to expand were reduced to driving herds over the Sierras into the Great Basin. A man named John Devine brought his blooded horses to Camp Smith (already abandoned by the army), built a quarter-mile racetrack, and settled alongside the all-season creek. Devine set a weather vane with a white horse atop the cupola on his barn, and named his new empire the Whitehorse Ranch.

That country was vastly isolated in those days, and still is. Out to the west is the Alvord Desert, a white playa in the rain shadow of the long ridge which is Steens Mountain. There is not much else to see.

But maybe John Devine knew what he was doing. He became a prince of the country, and he starts the history of settlement in that part of the world where my imagination still lives.

In 1872, Dr. Glenn put a twenty-three-year-old man named Peter French in charge of driving twelve hundred head of his Sacramento Valley cows north to the deserts of Oregon. French found the swamplands in the Blitzen Valley and the high summer range on Steens Mountain, and he claimed them, hauled saw-lumber fifty miles from a mill in the mountains to the north, built a white house, and began assembling the enormous P Ranch, which was arguably the finest natural set of livestock properties in the American West. Simple as that: this is mine. Soon the country was filling with settlers, white men and their families.

Late in the year that French was driving his cows to the Blitzen Valley, the Modoc War broke out south of Tule Lake on the Oregon-California border. A native named Captain Jack and around 175 of his Modoc followers holed up in a labyrinthine fortress of natural tunnels through the lava beds, and fought off the army until June 1, 1873. It was a little war, but it was an embarrassment to the military. Captain Jack was hanged at Fort Klamath, and afterward his body was dug up and embalmed and shown in carnivals all over the East Coast.

In the early part of 1873, Lieutenant Colonel Frank Wheaton, a commander in the District of the Lakes in southeastern Oregon, reports that a stock ranch in Warner Lakes Valley owned by D. R. Jones, eighteen miles from the post, was the nearest residence or settlement to Camp Warner. This makes D. R. Jones the first settler I know about in the valley where I grew up.

Sara Winnemucca was reported to be living with Mister Jones. Connections begin to accumulate.

In 1878, various native groups left the reservations and rose up in an outbreaking called the Bannock War; they killed Charlie On Long, a Chinese cook who worked for Peter French, and after that they lost and lost. The war was over within the year, and a considerable number of natives were herded together at old Fort Harney, east of Burns. Sara Winnemucca was among them.

On January 6, 1879, the women and old people and children were loaded into some fifty wagons, the men following on horseback, and escorted north through the terrible cold and the snows. A woman gave birth and the child died; the woman died a day later. Their bodies were left by the trail. Three children died of exposure as they traveled over two mountain ranges and the Columbia River to Fort Simcoe, just south of Yakima where my great-grandfather, Benjamin Franklin Kittredge, was the schoolteacher.

It was a Trail of Tears, yet I never heard it talked about in southeastern Oregon; I learned of it from books. It was not part of our common mythology. We knew a history filled with omissions, which can be thought of as lies. I wonder what my great-grandfather thought as those ruined Indians came to Fort Simcoe. I wonder if he saw them, if the children who survived entered his schoolroom, and what he did for them.

Sara Winnemucca was among her people the foremost woman of her time. In 1880 she was invited to visit Secretary of the Interior Carl Schurz in Washington, D.C., and she went. Sara wrote and published a book, *Life Among the Paiutes: Their Wrongs and Claims,* and she lectured in New York and Boston and Cambridge and Philadelphia, all on behalf of her tribe, but the government was finally not interested. So Sara went home, and in some metaphoric sense she went back to sleeping in blankets on the ground, with the traditional people. She died in October 1891. The official cause was too much wine. There was no mention of a broken heart.

Dr. Glenn ran for governor of California and was defeated.

Then one evening, out on the veranda porch at Jacinto, his formal house on the banks of the Sacramento River, he was shot to death by a drunken bookkeeper. Peter French married his daughter, Ella (who never lived with French in Oregon), accumulated an empire, and was shot dead by a small rancher in an argument over water. Glenn and French and Sara Winnemucca were people of vast energies and intelligence who died with their purposes in disarray; they wanted to move the world but it would not go.

My great-grandfather died the same year as Peter French, impoverished in Silver Lake. There was gold but he never found it. And anyway such riches were to have been only the beginning. The real treasures lay no doubt in some vision of easy fields greening up in spring, croplands flowing across the rolling plowground out back of the white-painted home place, and the gleeful crying of grandchildren at play on the lawns sloping to the mossy spring-creek—some particularly American version of promised-land solace. All this we promise you.

> Americans will not stand for the pioneer stuff, except in small sentimental doses. They know too well the grimness of it, the savage sight and savage failure which broke the back of the country but which also broke something in the human soul. The spirit and the will survived, but something in the soul perished; the softness, the floweriness, the natural tenderness. How could it survive the sheer brutality of the fight with that American wilderness, which is so big, vast, and obdurate? The savage America was conquered and subdued at the expense of instinctive and intuitive sympathy of the human soul. The fight was too brutal.
> —D. H. Lawrence,
> Introduction to Edward Dahlberg's *Bottom Dogs*

Lawrence goes on to talk of "an inward individual retraction, an isolation, an amorphous separateness like grains of sand, each grain isolated upon its own will." He laments "the breaking of the heart, the collapse of the flow of spontaneous warmth between a man and his fellows." He might have been writing directly about my people.

The settlers who came to that country were landless and transient and willing to live in isolation, driven by an urgency to accumulate properties—livestock before land, but always, in the long run, land. There weren't many of them, and though they lived far away from one another, at the end of some wagon track, each man inevitably knew every other man, by reputation anyway, across a territory measured in hundreds of miles, and any woman knew the other women. The isolation itself drove them to one another. Everybody got to share in the stories and what history there was.

It was history driven in part by a dream of some good society, even though many of the men weren't fit for society, or much interested. Nobody knows much about the women, and so far their stories have not been gathered. It was also history driven by an understanding of violence as a commonplace method of solving problems. Such things were talked about: *Take care of your people, take what you can, never give; let them push, and you will be pushed.* Everybody knew the rules, and the risks. Stories which constituted that history, at least in the beginning, were told with relish and candor.

But by my time, among the people who had got hold of some land, people with something to lose, a man who told stories was regarded as suspect and sappy. Perhaps people imagined that stories about the strength of ambition and will involved in climbing out of poverty were too lurid for polite mention. They turned closemouthed and secretive. For whatever reason, the stories died, and nobody told us anything revealing from the history of our family, or our neighbors' families. It was right there, as I understand it, that our failures, in my family, began. Without stories, in some very real sense, we do not know who we are, or who we might become. We were deprived like that.

In 1911 my grandfather borrowed money from his brother (at 12 percent—they never spoke after it was paid off) and bought a meadowland place called the River Ranch, on Ana River at the north end of Summer Lake. It was fine property if you could stand the horseflies in haying season. In 1916 he started summering cattle on the peat-bog marshlands along the Williamson River in the timbered mountains to the west, on the Klamath Indian Reservation. Soon he was buying in. One hard winter he got deed to 160 acres of good meadowland for a wagonload of groceries. Eventually my family owned something in excess of fifteen thousand acres on the Klamath Marsh.

He built a white house with a formal parlor and a polished staircase. Then the well went dry, so he jacked up the house, set it on rollers made of yellow pine logs, hitched a four-horse team to it, and took it up the country road a half-dozen miles to a point overlooking the Williamson River. The move took a couple of years. Nobody worked at it except in slack seasons; they lived in that house on the road, cooked in it, and slept in it, all the while. Imagine that white house, tall as a sailing ship, traffic detouring around, and the implacable man who was my grandfather. Those old bastards congregated in backcountry like ours, cherishing their own power of will, and their heedlessness, drawn to freedom they'd found by hiding out.

My grandfather, I think, came to feel he didn't have to discuss anything with anybody. Maybe he didn't want his motives examined; certainly he thought his will should prevail. Storytelling drifted to a stop. But like anyone, we wanted to live in a spiritually charged landscape; we wanted communal purposes. So we made them up for ourselves, over a couple of generations, reshaping the place where we lived. We tried to manage our ranchlands with efficiency we thought of as scientific, but our actual model was industrial. We worked hard to be analytic and coldhearted. The places around us were not alive with history but they could be useful. It was another way for the world to be dead.

It was a way of thinking which distanced us from everything we might have loved, like each other, and the place where we lived. No wonder so many of us (like myself) thought it would be easy to leave. I find myself searching for history out of books and dim remembrances, trying to fit it together in strings which reach from generation to generation, trying to loop myself into lines of significance.

In a family as unchurched as ours there was only one sacred story, and that was the one we told ourselves every day, the one about work and property and ownership, which is sad. We had lost track of stories like the one which tells us the world is to be cherished as if it exists inside our own skin. We were heedless people in a new country; we came and went in a couple of generations. But we plowed a lot of ground while we were there.

Now my mother is living out her life in a rest home in Salem, Oregon, and is pretty much bedbound. She is more than eighty years old, and seems to think the world is not likely to delight her with the things she always wanted (responsibility and respect, I think, more than anything). So she has withdrawn, and I respect her feelings. But she called me in when she heard I was writing about family.

"You have more than one family," she said, and she told me about some people named Obenchain, who came to Port Town-send, on Puget Sound, in 1862. She wanted to make it clear they were accomplished, some of them, and finely so. If I was a writer it was important I know about a great-great-aunt, a woman named Baker, who was widely published in popular magazines about a hundred years ago.

I think it is a story my mother got from her mother, one of the stories my mother told herself all her life, a story which sustained her, one of those stories which establish reasons for believing in your own excellent potentialities. I think that story was one of her solaces in life. I think she passed it along as a way of insisting on her own worth, and, in consequence, mine. And I thank her.

My mother, I have come to see, knows things I never imag-ined. She knows that knowing the story of your people in a kind of gossipy detail means you can name at least some of your most intimate connections to what has been called the blood of things. It means knowing the names of places, and who named them, and what happened there. In this way the incessant world is closer to becoming a territory where you might be able to take some rest.

John Charles Frémont came through our desert country with a troop of U.S. Army when it was almost entirely uninhabited by whites, during the winter of 1843, mapping, naming everything. They plowed through three-foot snowdrifts to reach a rim from which they looked down on green meadows alongside hot springs at the shore of an alkaline lake. Winter Rim and Summer Lake. A few days later they celebrated Christmas in Warner Valley, at a place called the Narrows, on a twisting waterway between swampy lakes where the Shoshones hunted. At their backs loomed the cliffs of Hart Mountain; those soldiers fired their howitzer into the falling snow and the thousands of waterbirds lifted to clamor in the wilderness sky; the soldiers drank their brandy and listened to the sighing of wings and must have known they hadn't mapped the significances of anything; such naming is not so easy.

But it's the way we make ourselves at home in the world, one act of the imagination after another, telling stories, naming: piss ants, remuda. In my schoolbooks as we idled along in the one-room Adel schoolhouse, I used to write Warner Valley, Lake County, Oregon, USA, World, Universe—wondering where it ended.

Such fantasies of connection drive my inclination to keep revisiting the high deserts of southeastern Oregon. I am continually trying to find some name for my dream. The long horizons of that country are imprinted in my synapses like a genetic heritage. It is the real world.

In the eye of my mind I see the enormous intricate dry watersheds that fan across southeastern Oregon more securely than the lines in the palms of my own hands. Twenty years in Montana, living in the rivercourse valleys through the northern Rockies, and the landscape there still seems like a toyland. In my bed before sleep I walk the lava-rock flats to stand on the rim overlooking the precise layout of cropland in Warner Valley.

CHAPTER 3

THE SHATTERED PIANO

> Writing a story or a novel is a way of discovering
> *sequence* in experience, of stumbling on cause
> and effect in the happenings of a writer's own
> life.
>
> —EUDORA WELTY,
> *One Writer's Beginnings*

When everything was *real*, we were tempted to say, talking about childhood. Rock climbers talk the same way about *exposure*, by which they mean the empty air beneath them, sometimes thousands of feet. "You're up there with all that exposure," one of them told me, when I asked him what he thought he was doing, courting risk up so high. "And even if you're roped and safe, you don't feel safe. So you're absolutely focused on the rock, you can't afford to think about anything *but* the rock, you can't let yourself hear an echo of anything but what you're doing, and for a while everything is *real*, all the distance is gone."

You have to wonder if he meant the world ceased—or at least seemed to cease, there for an extended moment—to be an act of the imagination. It's the dis-ease we all suffer from, so many of us, the fear that we can never really escape ourselves to know what is actual. And maybe it isn't a disease; it could be our true situation.

You have to wonder if the actual is what we so love about remembering childhood, or if we just love to remember our willingness, all that absorbed attention to fearless adventuring in the lands of the imagination. Or both. It's as if, when we are children, we understand that of course life is a storybook dream. And of course all of it is actual.

Our urge to detail the intimate particularities of the world we lived in as children is often, I suppose, a way of trying to return, to reconnect. If only we could find some trick by which we could be alive without the imagination standing between us and whatever is out there. Would we, then, ourselves, be as real as we were in that lost never-never land which we imagine as childhood before the fall, before the world went away into make-believe? And what about the idea that childhood is all make-believe? We feel so guilty; we know it is all our fault. As if we had any choice.

On bright afternoons when my people were scrambling to survive in the early days of the Great Depression, my mother, Josephine, was young and fresh as she led me on walks along the crumbling small-town streets of Malin, Oregon, in the Klamath Basin just north of the California border. I was three years old and understood what was actual as concentric circles of diminishing glory centered on the sun of her smile.

Outside our tight circle of complicity was my father, Oscar, that energetic stranger who came home at night and, before he touched anything, even me or my mother, rolled up his sleeves over his white forearms and scrubbed the stink of the turkeys off his hands in the kitchen sink with coarse gray Lava soap. Out beyond him was the world of the turkey herders, and beyond them lay the vast agricultural land of the Tule Lake Reclamation District, where they all worked.

What the herders did in the turkey business, as it was practiced by my father, was haul slatted chicken-wire crates full of turkeys around on old flatbed trucks. When they got to the backside of some farm property where nobody was likely to notice, they parked and opened those crates and turned the turkeys out to roam and feed on the grasshoppers. Occasionally they had permission, sometimes my father had paid a fee, and other times it was theft, grazing the turkeys for free. If they got caught, my father paid the fee; once in a while, they had to reload the turkeys into their crates and move on while some farmer watched with a shotgun.

My upbringing taught me to consider the barnyard turkey to be a captive, bitter, and rapacious creature, eyes dull with the opaque gleam of pure selfishness, without soul. I had never heard of a wild turkey. (Some part of our alienation, when we are most isolated, seems to me to be ecological. We are lonely and long to share what we regard as the dignity of wild animals—this is the phantom so many of us pursue as we hunt, complicating the actual killing into a double-bind sort of triumph.)

From the windows of our single-bedroom apartment on the second floor of the only brick building in Malin, where I slept on a little bed in the living room, we could look south across the rich irrigated potato and barley country of the Tule Lake Basin and see to California and the lava-field badlands where the Modoc Indians confronted the U.S. Army in the days of their rebellion.

I doubt if my mother told me about those natives in their

caves, but not because she didn't believe in storytelling. It's just that my mother would have told me other tales. She grew up loving opera. My grandfather (as I will always consider him, even though he was my mother's stepfather and we were not connected by blood) earned the money for her music lessons as a blacksmith for the California/Oregon Power Company in Klamath Falls. Sharpening steel, as he put it.

So it is unlikely my mother was fond of stories about desperate natives and holdout killings and the eventual hanging of Captain Jack, the Modoc war chief, at Fort Klamath. That was just the sort of nastiness she was interested in escaping. What my mother mainly told me about was Christmas as perfection realized: candied apples glowing in the light of an intricately decorated tree, and little toy railroads which tooted and circled the room as if the room were the world. And stories about Santa Claus.

But we live in a place more complex than any heaven we might imagine—some would say richer. The trouble began for me on a bright afternoon with a little skiff of snow on the ground, when my mother took me for my first barber shop haircut, an event which loomed large in our list of preparations for Christmas, and a step into manhood as she defined it.

I was enjoying the notion of such ceremony, and even the snipping of the barber's gentle shears as I sat elevated to manly height by the board across the arms of his chair—until Santa Claus came in, jerked off his cap and the fringe of snowy hair and his equally snowy beard, and stood revealed as an unshaven gray-faced man, who, from the way his hands were shaking, looked like he could stand a drink. He leered at my kindly barber, and muttered something. I suppose he wanted to know how long he would have to wait for a shave. Maybe he had been waiting all day; a brave, hung-over sort of waiting, all the while entombed in that Santa Claus suit. I screamed. I like to think I was screaming against chaos, in defense of my mother and notions of a proper Christmas, and maybe because this counterfeit Santa Claus, with his corded, unshaven neck, even looked remotely like a turkey as this remembering turns edgy and nightmarish and closer to make-believe.

The turkeys had been slaughtered the week before Thanksgiving in a couple of boxcars pulled onto a siding in Tule Lake, and shipped to markets in the East. Everyone who had worked for my father was at liberty and making ready to ride out winter on whatever they had managed to accumulate. So the party my parents threw on the night before Christmas meant the harvest was done, the turkeys were slaughtered, and the season of cold winds was truly begun. It was a time of release into meditation and winter, to await rebirth. As I recall from this distance this was a party for the turkey herders, those men who had helped my father conspire his way through that humiliating summer with those terrible creatures. At least the faces I see in my dream of that yellow kitchen are the faces of those men. Never again, said my mother, and my father agreed that better times were coming, and everybody got drunk.

I had been put down to sleep on the big bed in my parents' bedroom, which was quite a thing in itself. It was only late in the night that I woke to a sense of something gone wrong. The safe place where I lived with my mother had been invaded by laughter and hoedown harmonica music and boots stomping and people dancing.

Nobody saw me for a long moment as I stood in the doorway from the bedroom into the kitchen in my pajamas. Not until I began my hysterical momma's-boy shrieking. The harmonica stopped, and my mother looked shamefaced at me from the middle of the room where she had been dancing with my father while everyone watched. All those people, who are mostly dead, turned to me, and it was as if I had gotten up and come out of my parents' bedroom into a leering nightmare, vivid light and whiskey bottles on the table and faces glazed with grotesque intentions.

Someone saved it, one of the men, maybe my father, by picking me up and ignoring my wailing as the harmonica music started again, and then I was in my mother's arms as she danced, whirling around the kitchen table and the center of all attention in a world where everything was possible and all right while the turkey herders watched and thought their private thoughts, and it was Christmas at last, in my mother's arms.

In all that life there was a kind of readiness and wildness. My mother was working for the Ford dealer in Klamath Falls when she met my father. She says he came in unshaven and obviously hung over after a poker game of several days' duration, thirty-one years old and never married or close to it. He tossed out a wadded pocketful of folding money he'd won, and told her he wanted a Ford, right away. "Well," she told me, "a man like that caught your eye."

My father continued to run at life in that heedless way, much to the consternation of his father, but the work got done. A man with an almost infinite capacity for loyalty, my father kept his friends around him, and cut them in on the action as much as he could.

For years the faces of those men in that bright kitchen were part of dreams I dreaded as I tried to go to sleep. In struggling against my fear of them I was making a start toward learning to create distance between myself and people I should have cared for. Eventually my mother put me back to my sleep and now I am here, wishing I could remember those men in some more specific way because they are so deeply toward the heart of what I have to celebrate, and yet mostly lost to me, except for this story.

By the next spring, 1937, everything had changed. My grandfather was buying the MC Ranch in Warner Valley. The deal represented an enormous change in our fortunes. He signed the legal papers and took possession of those fields and distances as his own with no money down when he was sixty-two years old. He pledged everything he had worked for all his life, unable to resist such a kingdom.

My father went into business with him. He was gone to Warner most of the time, surveying the possibilities, making his plans, and supervising the building of our new house. All at once he had a line of credit as long as his arm. My mother and I spent the summer in a rented single-bedroom place on Third Street in Klamath Falls (where, in spring sunlight, I first saw my father naked). Our new house was finished in the fall, and we moved.

My mother had come to marriage with a lot of fine furniture. The furniture was loaded on a ranch truck, to be driven to the ranch in Warner by an employee and drinking crony of my father's, a man named Jack Ray. We were to follow. It seemed to a child that we drove all day, and then we came to our wreck. Beyond the lumber-milling town of Bly, the farm truck had overturned down in the juniper trees, so far from the narrow asphalt highway we almost didn't notice. Jack Ray had been at the whiskey, and my mother's furniture, including her black grand piano, was mostly a collection of splintered hardwood.

Served her fair enough, some people thought, like my grandmother on my father's side, who considered hauling a piano out to the ranch an act of arrogance. I like to imagine the sounds of those piano wires snapping and twanging as the wreck settled, and Jack Ray rubbing his head and feeling around in the upside-down truck for his pint. Jack Ray wasn't hurt. My father said Jack would die in bed, and he did.

That wreck cast a considerable shadow. My grandfather followed strict rules, one of which was *Never hire the people you drink with.* Through loyalty to old friends, my father had made a philosophical mistake. Maybe it was just that his eldest-son arrogances had finally caught up and come home. Implications reverberated all down the line. To this day my mother hates the thought of Jack Ray. When I reminded her of Jack recently, she almost spat. "That damned fool," she said.

My mother eventually got another piano, and she never lost her belief that art and music could survive the ranching life she had come to when she married my father. But that wreck seemed to prove that my grandfather was correct in his bottom-line way of understanding the world, and that my mother and her piano and all it stood for were mostly pointless, and a pain in the neck. It was a point of view that prevailed for a long time.

Not so long ago I went back to Warner. When I came to the apple trees behind the house where we lived it was as if the child within me had forgotten nothing. I could remember which way to climb, which limbs, and where to sit, up there, so no one could see you as you looked out across the valley. I loved it again, as you would if it was your home through the years of your upbringing, and the early lives of your own children.

As I regard these memories I can begin to smell summertime, and I can hear the buzzing of the yellow jackets as they went after the ripe fruit in our little grove of plum brush. I want these memories to become increasingly dense and real, hoping they are mostly not make-believe. They are dear to me, and essential in my attempts to name what is most valuable. If these are not real, I am lost.

In midsummer, far out in the valley, in early morning, thin clouds of dust would be rising to the sky above the hay-camp corrals where our mowing and stacking crews were catching their work teams and harnessing them and feeding them a bait of oats before breakfast. Eventually the meadows of the Thompson Field, just below our house, would be mowed and windrowed, and the cured hay would be run over the beaver slides and stacked in the stackyards. My father would take me down to the fields, and I would watch the men at their work and know it would be mine to do someday. That was the mythology: there would come a day when I would be responsible for the work. Sure enough, it came.

By mid-September the leaves would be turning in the orchard, and on the Lombardy poplars which boxed our yard. Those old trees were planted when settlers first came to the valley in the decades before 1900. They were wonderfully valuable to our lives, the poplars and twenty or so apple trees of the most hardy varieties and three pear trees which blossomed every year but only once in a while brought any fruit. That was all right. They defined our garden. Only a fool cuts down a tree in that country.

Warner Valley, when I was prime in my readiness to witness paradise, was in what I think of as its prelapsarian stage, an oasis in a country where the water doesn't run to any sea. It was clear we had stumbled on to a mostly untouched place, and rare good fortune.

The people who brought us there, my grandparents on my

father's side of our family, were imperious and heedless; they came from poverty on the high deserts. My grandmother dried her wash on a barbed wire fence around an unpainted house until her children were mostly grown. My grandfather was a hard-shell desert cattle rancher. For decades he summered alone on the deserts east of Silver Lake, isolated and tending his cattle.

His early years were devoted to an often brutal horseback notion of life; he felt he had earned what he had, and he was right. But the earning had hardened him and he was absorbed with ambition. Running his properties on borrowed money, he wanted more. It was his theory that for the common good we should put work ahead of every other thing, including compassion, and for a long time my family tried to live by that theory. If you paid the bills, in the philosophy he taught, you got to call the shots.

Accumulation was my grandfather's game, and he had standards; he wanted things done correctly. In his story, if we took enough care and sacrificed enough—and here the story goes sideways—we would eventually get to live in town most of the year, as he did, in a big rock-walled house, and own linens and painted china and silver tableware. Correct was part of secure, and at the heart of actual. It was a story he wanted to believe, and one he used to manipulate everyone. He got away with it for most of his life. He was not so much cruel as indifferent to purposes other than his own, and mainly interested in his cattle and how they were doing, beef on the hoof, for sale.

For my grandfather, in that beginning, Warner must have been the ultimate answer to a lifetime of yearning, thousands of acres of meadow on the high side of the valley, cut with sloughs and willows for shelter, where he could winter his stock on native hay stacked with the beaver slides. Experienced men said the MC was the finest ranch property they'd ever seen.

My grandparents, so long as they had any choice, were never

going back to the high deserts. They clearly knew that they were living in a dream which had come to them at least partway through luck. Right then they were having the good luck of cheap land in the Great Depression, and later on they would have the good luck of terrific grain prices during World War II.

But they also understood that most of their luck had come as a result of their own invention and sharp dealing, and they were pretty much justified in thinking they had made their own way. My grandfather had early on come to understand that a reputation for hard work and a kind of calculated recklessness, along with an absolute willingness to pursue litigation, could get you a long way with certain bankers. So long as they trusted one another inside the family, which wasn't even a couple of decades, their luck ran to aces for all of us. By the time it broke I should have been gone into my own enterprises; it is my own fault, and misfortune, that I wasn't.

An ancient world was changing, and my people were on the leading edge of the conversion. They not only knew it, but also gloried in it. The idea that they were connected to important doings and improvements in the world inhabited them and drove them forward.

Thirty-six miles of washboard gravel county road twisted over the Warner Mountains to end with us; to the east, wagon roads twisted among the rimrocks and alkali flats, but essentially the way into our valley was the way out. There was no electricity but our own, generated for house lights by the Delco power plant with its rows of glass batteries, and no functioning telephone at all, although sometime in the past there had been. In the Adel Store an old hand-crank instrument hung on the wall, and telephone wire dangled from a line of spindly home-cut jack-pine poles along the road to town.

In February and early March the creeks draining out of the Warner Mountains to the west, Deep Creek and Twenty Mile Creek, would flood and fill the vast tulebeds until at sunset the swamps on the far east side of the valley would shimmer with water like a lake. The unbroken peat soil under those miles of swamp was eight feet deep in places.

The point here is abundance, an overwhelming property thronging with natural life, and what my family did with it. My grandfather wondered how such a place could best be used. My father tried to show him. That was probably my father's main lifetime mistake, making any effort at all to live in his father's life. But they were family, and my father saw that valley as possibility. Oscar Kittredge had been to school at the Oregon Agricultural College in Corvallis; he was an engineer, one of the new men, a visionary.

He bought a cable-drum Caterpillar RD-6 track layer fitted out with a bulldozer blade, which he used to start building a seventeen-mile diversion levee to carry the spring flood waters of Twenty Mile Creek north along the east side of the valley, to drain our swamplands. Seventeen miles. In those times such a project was considered insanely ambitious.

My father was the joke of the country, but not for long. He jury-rigged a generator and battery system to run off the diesel engine of that RD-6, mounted it with lights, and ran it at the levee site twenty-four hours a day, summer and winter, except for fuel stops and maintenance. Then he bought an RD-7, and used it to build his levee while he started plowing the tulebeds with the RD-6, also twenty-four hours a day.

Near as I can fix them, from conversations with my mother, these next memories come from the summer of 1937. My father was making ready to start the harvest of his first bumper crop of oats off the hundreds of acres already broken out into plowground. My mother was his bookkeeper and main factotum.

One of her duties involved driving out to cross the natural drainage on the east side of the valley at a place called the Beatty Bridge, and out through the greasewood wastelands along the high-ground edges of the swamps to a cluster of abandoned homestead buildings known as the Fee Place, where my father had established his farming and catskinners' camp and cookhouse. My mother had to make the run every couple of days, carrying spare parts and groceries.

It was summer and hot, but my mother would stop after we came off the Beatty Bridge and roll up all the windows. Then she would rev the engine on the old black Buick she drove to her work, sweat already accumulating on her upper lip, and we would plunge off into the alkali dust which would rise around us like something alive from the deeply eroded roadway through the greasewood. My mother drove fast, holding her breath, as if speed could be a way of escape. The long roostertail of dust we raised hung visible in the morning air for a half hour. Down there in our Buick, that part of the trip was like a passage through darkness for me and, I'm sure, my mother. No matter how tightly the windows were sealed, the fine dust sifted inside like water.

We would come out onto the rocky shale of a slight rise to the Fee Place, and the air would clear and we would be safe for a while, until we had to start back. We would roll down the windows and the dust would flow off the windshield like water and my mother would lick her upper lip, and I would realize how childish I had been, frightened of dust.

The high ground at the Fee Place had been an old camping ground for the Paiutes and Modocs and Klamaths. They must have camped there over centuries, hunting the waterbirds and gathering native grains from the swamps. My mother would banter with the camp cook—I remember a sour-smelling young woman named Ida—and drink a couple of cups of coffee while I hunted the high ground for arrowheads, which I found by the pocketful. But what I most vividly recall from those early trips to the Fee Place was looking out across the raw sixteen-foot berm of earth which was the diversion levee. Beyond lay the plowground, where the bright seedlings of my father's oat crop were emerging from the earth in long undulating drill rows.

My mother and that camp cook named Ida, both of them in thin summery yellow dresses, their arms bare in the sunlight, came out to stand below me, shading their eyes and gazing in the direction I was looking, talking and nodding. I cannot imagine what they might have been looking toward as they stand blessing this memory of the degree to which we all believed in one another in those days.

My father raised the heaviest oats produced anywhere in America on that new ground, or so he told me, according to what buyers told him. It was probably a common phenomenon. Somebody was always breaking out new ground, and for a couple of years their crops were the finest anywhere in America.

Every so often one of the women would organize a family get-together, usually at one of the cookhouses. At precisely six o'clock, summer or winter, the cook would clang the dinner bell and we would troop in and seat ourselves down both sides of a long table with the workmen. My grandfather was always at the head of the table, with my grandmother beside him. And there was me and my father and mother and my brother and sister, and a mix of aunts and uncles and cousins.

I try to imagine what we looked like, the owners of the

property and their wives and children, there in the late 1930s, at the heart of the Great Depression, laughing and confident as we passed the platters of boiled beef and the bowls of mashed potatoes and gray milk gravy. Some of the workmen would be too shy to talk, eyeing the women as if they were creatures who had just come from another planet. I wonder how many of those men despised us, and if they understood that they did, or why. There was a kind of complaint you would hear at that table in the days afterward, something like this: "Goddamn a woman. All that goddamned talk. You got to sit there and listen. You might say 'shit' so you can't say a goddamned thing."

Times were poor, but the men in my family were capable of supporting women and children; they owned the biggest ranch in that country. Those were the essentials of power, and they were on exhibition. Blame it on women. But it was not women, they weren't the real complaint. It was what those women represented: power and civility and the possibility of love, or at least affection and family. Those were the things we were supposed to be sharing when we went to eat in the cook-houses, and maybe even a little of the power. But never money. Some of those men must have sensed that those meals were a fraud. Nobody was actually sharing anything.

It must have been my grandfather's idea that we should sit down with the men who worked for us and eat what they ate, off tin plates. No doubt he passed it off as a way of staying in touch with our beginnings, another way of taking care. But in retrospect those meals look like self-serving political bullshit designed to reveal our family as common and decent. They look as if they might have been designed to breed loyalty among the workmen, and to feed the family ego. We were poor people who had risen; we were naming ourselves.

It is an old story. If the ruling class observes certain decencies, everything might last forever. My people may have believed such things; maybe they believed in magic, maybe not. But the power of money over love ultimately generated seemingly inevitable troubles among people who started out trying to care for one another, fathers and sons, women and the men they married. It was a sorry legacy. By the time I was grown my father had stopped speaking to his father, and my mother had left them both behind.

Just before Christmas of 1937, during a visit to my maternal grandparents' house, the two-bedroom house where my mother grew up on Jefferson Street in Klamath Falls, there came irrevocable change. I have not been inside that house in forty years and now it is torn down, but I recall the look of the stillness, and the quiet as my grandparents went about their strategies of avoiding each other, the gray floral wallpaper, the trapdoor which lifted up in the kitchen floor to reveal the steep unpainted stairs down into the dark, earthen-floored little cellar where my grandfather brewed his beer.

It began innocently. I remember sunlight on the aging yellow wallpaper in the front bedroom where my grandmother slept until we came to visit, my terrible headache—the beginning of what I took to be an ordinary illness—and lie-about days during which my mother and grandmother spent their attentions on no one but me. It was perfect. My father was gone to wherever he always went, my maternal grandfather doted on me, and I had the women captured by my incapacity. In such models we find our lives if we aren't careful.

But this was polio. My next memories have to do with glimpses of winter sunlight through evergreens outside the train compartment as we rushed north through the Cascade Mountains to Portland. The world had gone hallucinatory. I see an ambulance meeting the train late at night. My mother says there was no ambulance, no strobe flashing down the length of the wet dark tracks beyond the yellow lights in the coaches. Maybe she's right.

For an hour or so each day, my mother was allowed to visit in an undecorated green-walled private room in a hospital somewhere in Portland. My father is not in these memories at all. Maybe he had gone home to Warner Valley and his work. I don't recall noticing his absence. But my mother, that was another thing. I was five years old, and not so much terrified when she left as hypnotized by loss, filled with hatred of the universe in its perfect unfairness. Something terrible was happening and I was not being allowed even the solace of my only love.

The world would not yield to my powers; I would howl until I was exhausted. The nurses shut the door to my room and left me to my steadfast rage. That failure of my will to carry the world, and my isolation into powerlessness, was profoundly worse than any incapacity connected to my illness. Polio was only crippling. Lions circled in my dreams, night after night, in a room I visited only in those dreams, a room where everything valuable (little pots and figurines) was put up on a high shelf, out of my reach.

Eventually my mother took me south to San Francisco and the Shriners' Crippled Children's Hospital on Nineteenth Avenue, into a ward with children in my same condition. It was said I would be happier, and I was. There were peacocks in a garden just out my window, and I was getting better. My mother brought me a toy grocery store with little shelves and counters and boxes of soap to sell. I set up my shop when she was not there, and talked to myself about selling things. It was real as life. I forgot my mother for hours, lapses for which I despised myself. The nurses said I was becoming a little man. I knew it was a lie. What I was, and didn't tell anyone, was a broken thing, forced to live in make-believe.

Then I discovered that my terrible dreams about lions would stop if I was careful not to go to sleep with my head on my arm. I was hearing the rush of my own blood in my dreams; that was the roaring. If I slept with the pillow between my head and my arm, everything would be fine; the lions would not prowl in my night, the world would not be lost. I still sleep that way.

It is a discovery I recall with absolute clarity. I told my mother, and I think she wept over me. But I was not crazy. From then on, with religious fervor, I knew I was going to be all right, never a doubt. In my childlike way I had come to an understanding that the world can be lived in as one act of the imagination after another, and that much of what you are capable of imagining can become real.

Soon I was back home in Klamath Falls, up on the cold hardwood floors in the cold rooms of my grandfather's rock-walled house with my cousins, attempting to balance one lettered block on another, and another on that, so they would spell something and be whole. A little boy, they said, with such courage. The polio was gone, as if magically. There was a time when I could not stack the blocks one on top of the other, and then I was recovered and running the sandy trails through the sage on the foothills in Warner Valley with no aftereffects at all, as if some deal had been struck with the Devil. My mother kept me from beginning the first grade in the Adel School that fall, thinking I needed time to complete my recovery, and I hated her; I'd had enough of isolation.

So my grandparents on my mother's side, inland people all their lives, took me on a trip over Greensprings Mountain and down through the valleys around Medford and Grants Pass, to the dunelands of the Oregon coast. I recall nothing from my first sight of the Pacific. What I remember is a crab leg on the beach, a wonderful toy, at once mechanical and reeking with the mystery of death and the sea. I could make the pincers open and close by pulling a tendon, and pinch my grandmother.

My memory of that crab leg, of the smell and slant of seawind and offshore rain, and my sense of those old people in their bemused decency again convince me that the world is so simple a thing, and coherent. Is that sentimentality?

But at the time I hated them, as my mother reminds me. My crab leg stank. They tossed it out, and I sailed flat stones at them with a mean limber wing, hard as a boy can throw. I meant to do them damage. So they shook their heads, and for that season washed their hands of my salvation. They took me home to the loneliness of preschool afternoons in Warner Valley, where I would learn to *see*, which became another solution, another victory.

I was alone. My brother was only four; my sister was an infant. I had nobody my age to travel with, but I don't think I cared. (My brother and sister don't much exist in these early memories; people tell me this is universal, younger siblings seeming simply unreal.) I wonder if the oldest child is always such a solo act, learning to inhabit an ego which is always attempting to be untouchable.

What my mother thought I needed, near as I can figure, was some little-boy time in the world. After lunch she would pour oats to rattle in a gallon can and help me catch and saddle my old horse Snip, and boost me into the saddle. I would roam the sandhills below the rim back of our house, up to the old Indian graveyard where half the graves had been dug up by vandals and the wooden headmarkers were mostly knocked down and scattered into the brush. Whatever was written on them had long since weathered into illegibility. The Indian graveyard was the far edge of my territory. From there I could look down on our green-roofed house, watching the women who worked for my mother as they pinned wash to the line.

When I wasn't horseback I would wander on foot and learned to move like a small stalking beast along the brushy paths through the willows down in the Thompson Field, looking for quail in the thickets. Everything was changing. I was learning to connect with the specific world in its intricacies. Things were actual and stank and some would chew your finger if given half a chance; just stick your finger down a badger hole to find out.

A child's strict attentiveness was what I had been tricked into giving. I climbed out onto the high limbs of our crabapple tree, where they reached above the rooftops, and let my mother search for me while I went on studying the bright green- and vividly orange-striped caterpillars as they ate the leaves. I think I heard their chewing, and later on, down in the meadows, I know I heard the rasping of snakes passing through the meadow grass. I was a spy, following Charlie Craig, the old man my father hired to work the huge kitchen garden, as he farted along between the rows on his hands and knees, picking cucumbers.

Distance was part of what I was really practicing while I imagined I was educating myself in the secrets of animals. I would lift weathered planks and catch a writhing little mass of pink hairless baby field mice in their nests. Maybe a sense of forbidden intimacy was part of my passion toward what is called *knowing* the world as I killed those mice in a private little fever. I stabbed a tame duck with a kitchen knife, and it died. Something was wrong with me, I knew, and I was right. There was an animal inside me that didn't know what to do.

My prelapsarian kingdom came to its end, I think, along

about then. I shudder at memories of that child stabbing the duck, but I mourn the loss of what I take to be intimacy with the living world. Occasionally I like to imagine I will take the time to reconnect in that way, as if time spent courting the world in its slow complexities would change everything. No matter how much time I take, I find it impossible to dissolve into the dreams of the spider in her web.

At last my mother relented, deciding, I imagine, that I was more trouble out of school than I was worth, and I was sent off into schoolboy crushes and shouting and learning to emulate the big kids as they warred on each other with what were called "rubber guns," hair-triggered weapons which could raise a welt at twenty yards with the heavy stinging bands of rubber they shot, cut from old truck-tire inner tubes. That fall in the Adel schoolyard the creation of rubber guns was our sole obsession. Then it was winter and we all learned harmonica and had harmonica bands. In the spring we learned quick-draw with toy six-shooters and live snapping caps. Rubber guns were long forgotten.

The world turned slow again in summer, but I was never so alone as I had been that couple of months while my mother held me out of school to recover from polio. My second year in school I learned to draw pictures of an island which rose up from the ocean with unclimbable walls. There was a path to the house at the top in that picture, but no people whatsoever. I drew it over and over because I could always get it right. They say we learn to name ourselves as a single entity by looking in the mirror and realizing we are distinct from every other thing.

My grandfather believed in property, and, given any excuse, he labored seven days a week. Raised poor, and likely humiliated by the failures of a father who wasted himself in a wandering, fortune-seeker's life, it's possible that in the beginning what he hungered for was the direct simplicity of work as an escape from that humiliation. Later in life he seemed driven to keep on proving himself. He wanted to assemble an empire, and love was not much of a consideration inside our family so long as he was calling the shots. Maybe love was not very real to him; what he demanded was dedication to his purposes, and obedience.

"Whenever we got ahead," my grandmother lamented after he was dead, "we bought land." Artists say they are trying to create a thing that will endure. Some say they think of it as a way of defeating death. It's possible those ranches were my grandfather's art, although you can't help but be suspicious of such off-the-cuff psychoanalyzing. In any event his properties didn't much outlast him.

My father was a more generous kind of animal, and thought you could mix in some good times along the way. He loved to play. The earliest of his frolicking that I know about involved Henry Nicol, a huge dark-faced man, rumored to be half Indian, who was my father's best friend from the time before either one was married. Nick and Oscar, it was said, they were a pair to draw to. They would take a month in late May and early June, and hike to the fishing lakes high in the Cascades, packing nothing but blankets and fly rods and salt and vinegar and a slab of bacon. There would be two feet of snow. Nick and Oscar would toss their blankets down into the hollow next to the trunk of a big yellow pine, and bed there and be warm enough, smelling the beauty as they slept. They would never want to come home.

Nick married my father's younger sister, Marie. She died of pneumonia the winter of 1931. Their child, my cousin Jack, was an infant, and my grandparents took him to raise, which was a common thing in those days. After Nick remarried, to a vivid redheaded woman named Nellie, and moved to Warner to lease farming land from my father, Jack didn't go back to live in his father's home. I don't know why.

Each Fourth of July, as a way of reliving old times, and as an escape from the heat of the desert country, my father and Nick would haul a load of us up into the Cascades for a week at Odell Lake. We'd set up camp in a series of rough cabins which were called Millionaires Row, thirteen board and batten cabins (four or six rented just for our people) strung along under the yellow-bellied ponderosa pines on the south bank of Odell Creek. My brother and sister and cousins and I would wade the cold water of the creek, turning rocks and hunting hellgrammites in their sandy little sheaths, making ready for our main business of the outdoor day, which was killing fish.

The lakeside docks, worn by the pounding of winter waters, were mossy and ancient as fundamental stone. (I am shocked to know they have been torn out and replaced for thirty years.) Those children were willing and guiltless, and their world's record was 132 glimmering little inedible suckers in one day. We filled buckets with them. The adults would not even help with the counting. They had their own records to set, and I ached to join them in their going.

The summer of 1938 I was six years old and the only child who would walk the four or so miles up to Rosary Lake on the ridge of the Cascades, a tiny lake formed by a geologically recent rockslide, where enormous trout were rumored to live. Rosary was a word that had something to do with God, and it seemed right. We floated calmly on jury-rigged rafts, ours held together by a pair of suspenders. The gray craggy rocks, rising around us spirelike to the sky, were like churches in a row. Far down in the clear water we could see tree stumps lifting toward us. Moving among them were so-called pan-size trout, who ignored our bait although they fed eagerly on the milky drift of canned corn some of the adults were dumping as chum. But nobody spotted any secret monsters. By early afternoon I was bored and Nellie Nicol and I walked out the four miles down the trail. The men were going to hang on for the evening hatch.

All I recall of that walk through the Douglas fir forest is the shimmering sounds of afternoon, and my sense that the adults had betrayed me by turning out to be boring. Which was how things stood until I came awake late in the night to find the men were home, drinking and a little drunk around the fire, talking and showing their big fish from Rosary Lake. The sides of those huge trout flared silvery against the firelight, secret fish from deep amid the roots still rotting out on the bottom, chummed up with corn to feed in the oncoming darkness, and I once again believed in the power of adults.

Lately I have been studying that day in photographs. I am years older than those people were then in their mysteries, on their blankets by the stream, in their deceptions, drinking their whiskey. They frighten me yet, with their powers. They were not like us. In my childhood, surrounded by those men and women, it seemed they were like nature.

Someone told me that Henry Nicol, after his heart started going bad, spent some hours in the third-story attic of my grandparents' rock-walled house in Klamath Falls on a winter night, going through a trunk of Marie's clothes, the fabric of old-fashioned dresses in his hands as he lifted them to his face and perhaps tried to sense that she might still exist in an odor, and reassure himself that the things he remembered were actual and had happened once. It was as close, I think, as anything in that crowd came to praying. Maybe it's near to what I'm attempting here.

Early on I came to the idea that my parents were cultured beyond the average run in matters of taste and insight. It was of
enormous importance to me as I came to understand that I had
inherited the right to pick between more lives than one.

That sense of my parents started, I think, with my mother
and her pianos and singing lessons. She got me through only
three piano lessons the summer I was six; I hated her for them.
Then they sent me away to school. For reasons I was never
clear about—something to do with classroom advantages is the
way it was put to me—I spent the spring of 1941 with my mother's parents on Jefferson Street in Klamath Falls, walking a couple of blocks to the Frémont School.

This was my first exposure to the life of city boys. The
children of my mother's old high school friends befriended me.
As children are, I was acutely worried about looking right, and
knowing who was best friends with whom, and what each had
to do with the other. I fell in love with a pretty doll-faced girl
named Rosemary. All my friends were in love with Rosemary.
My mother's mother dressed me in freshly ironed, clean-smelling
clothes every day, I fussed over the roll of curl in my hair as I
combed it incessantly, and I loved becoming a sweet, soft little
fop. Nobody at the Adel School got to do such things, and I
must have been an odd creature when I went home to summer
on the ranch. Maybe I had always been privileged and strange.

My mother had been taking my brother and sister and me
to San Francisco since I was a small child. I remember foggy
nights on Treasure Island, at the Golden Gate International Ex-
position in 1939, watching some kind of Buffalo Bill Golden
West Horse-O-Rama, wagon trains, Custer galloping to victory

over the Indians, all of it. Those trips were understood as befitting for the children of ranchland aristocracy, and particularly important to my father's children.

It was part of our family mythology, a story it seems like I always knew, that the most important single event in my father's life turned around a conversation he had with his father in the mid-1920s. My father had graduated from Oregon Agricultural College in Corvallis, and had come home to the ranch on the Klamath Marsh to work out the summer before law school. His father took him out to privacy on the front porch of the white house above the creek, and they spent the day, my grandfather persuading and my father resisting until his resistance broke and he gave up his notion of studying law and pledged himself to stay home and take up his responsibilities on the property. It was a decision my father regretted all his life. His ultimate weakness before his father's persuasion had a lot to do with the hatred that developed between them in the long run.

So it was important to my father that his children have every opportunity to go on toward what he saw as the possibility of a larger life, beyond ranching. He sent me to Menlo School for part of my senior year, thinking a private school education would help get me into Stanford. And I'm sure it would have. He was offering another life, one he wanted and missed, focused on the ideal of Stanford Law School, but I didn't want Stanford and ran home to high school in Klamath Falls. I wanted Oregon State and my own kind. He dismissed me, and turned his ambitions toward my brother, Pat. And that didn't work out either.

My mother saw to it her children were raised in the traditions of country money; she bought me English wingtip shoes and a tweed suit for my months in the seventh grade at Tamalpais. My mother and my brother and my sister and I lived for

weeks at a time in the old Plaza Hotel on the north side of
Union Square in San Francisco; we ate in hotel restaurants,
bought flowers from florists in the lobby. It might seem we
were raised in a worldly way, but we remained isolated if not
innocent.

Neither of my parents explained the ways power and money
work in the world. Surely, if we knew who we should be, or
what to want, we would tell our children. Or maybe not? For
a long time, I saw my mother and father going about their lives
with what seemed such assurance, and wondered why they had
never told me anything actually useful. My mother must have
thought such explanations were my father's job. I was a smart-
assed kid and my father a man of circumstance. Maybe it seemed
impossible to set me down for a talk without seeming to reenact
that scene out on the porch at the Klamath Marsh with his own
father. Anyway, what do you say? Do you tell your son, "Don't
live like I did"? I think the answer is yes you do, as he did,
eventually.

My sister and my brother and I were not educated to ne-
gotiate anything of the slightest slippery importance. We have
lived reckless and haphazard lives. Maybe it was because we
were allowed to believe we had options that would never run
out, and that might only be a way of saying we lacked the
common sense to attempt cleverness. And maybe we're better
off in the long run, if that's not too self-justifying, even as I keep
trying to fault someone. Maybe it's just that the world beyond
our deserts was as fundamentally mysterious to my parents as it
was to us.

In the way of people gone to the backlands, carrying hardwood
furniture to some metaphoric wilderness, my family liked to

think of themselves as practiced in customs brought along from that other country where they originated, where propriety ruled, or so they imagined: the East. *We might be reinventing the wilderness, but we are acquainted with civilities and with taking care of traditions.*

Distantly related aunts and uncles and nieces and nephews would come to visit from faraway seaports like Boston. Probably they came because we lived in the Far West on a cattle ranch the size of Delaware, inhabiting a cowboy romance, but they came. There was a rear admiral, a specialist in naval history who wore tweeds in the summertime, and pale thin women with rimless eyeglasses who draped themselves with silk scarves. They did not want to see the fields. "Too dusty, don't you imagine?"

They spent all their daylight time at the ranch in my mother's living room, with the shades drawn, playing bridge. I can see them, motes of dust floating in shafts of midafternoon sunlight. After they were gone my mother was outraged, looking to my father for confirmation. "Aren't they pitiable?" She so clearly thought hers was the right life. My father shrugged, but he must have agreed. They were his family, but he had never stayed home while they were visiting.

My cousin Michael came from San Francisco, where his father owned a private school. Mike spent two or three summers in the hayfields, learning to harness a team, set nets for the haystacking crew, and swallow discomfort. He never got very good at it. He complained, and would not, we knew, ever come to much.

Mike has been dead of cancer for more than a decade, and I didn't know it for years. I learned of it only by accident from some friends in San Francisco. In the late 1960s Mike was a figure of some power in the public school system in the Bay Area, and my friends had despised him for his conservatism, which they understood as racist. They asked if we were related, and seemed to almost relish the fact of his death. I didn't know if I should try to defend him or not; I hadn't thought of Mike since 1965, when he came through southeastern Oregon with his wife and a home-built plywood bar in the trunk of his car. We stood in the parking lot at the Lakeview Lodge Motel, and he mixed us some martinis while we took the air on a hot midsummer evening. Mike and I got a little drunk, and I liked him fine. That was the last of those family visits from some distant place, so far as I know. By then we had lost contact, not only with our connections to the so-called great world outside southeastern Oregon, but with each other.

A memory I love begins on a Sunday evening, in the little house where Henry Nicol lived with his redheaded second wife, Nellie, who was widely regarded as a sport. She must have been, it was said, or she would never have married Nick. My father and mother are there and they are all drinking, telling stories and singing, and the smoky air is thick with camaraderie; they are bandits around the fire.

Part of Nick's style was familiarity with art and Shakespeare. On Sunday afternoons, while pitch logs snapped, he would quote poetry. Nobody can recall just which Shakespeare it was, but it was poetry and they liked the fact that he had it by heart, and that he was willing to recite it for them when the time was right.

On those evenings my father and Nick would continue a long-running quarrel over Charlie Russell. There were maybe a half-dozen framed Russell prints around on the walls, and those pictures were taken seriously and praised for their accuracy. You could read the brands on the horses. They were real brands, not just something the painter made up. "True to life" was the ultimate test of artistic worth. What it amounted to, I think, was the fact that these were country people who didn't know much about painting but loved the idea that somebody had taken their part of the world so seriously. Wouldn't most of us find pride in the idea that a famous artist like Charlie Russell had focused a lifetime of attention on our part of creation? And that he cared enough to get everything right? That was important, getting everything right.

The subject of the debate between my father and Nick was a picture of a stagecoach holdup. The stage had come down a draw, and some holdup men had appeared out of the rocks with their guns drawn. That was it. The stage was standing with its doors open, its passengers being robbed under a rising sun. Or was it a brilliant moon? Or the setting sun? That was the question, debated with lots of high mock seriousness and betting and a letter to Charlie Russell that never got mailed to my knowledge, and likely was never written because Charlie Russell had been dead for years. But Nick and Nellie and Jo and Oscar, they were eager to care because they loved each other. That was the point—their lives were thick with consequence because of that love. As mine would be. I was their fortunate child. It was a long time before it occurred to me that maybe they understood all that Charlie Russell talk as tomfoolery.

About a quarter mile down the sage hillslope toward the hay-field meadows of the Thompson Field, there was a house where the crazy woman lived with her overgrown, crazy son, who was my forbidden friend. I wasn't allowed to play with him, but I rode down anyway on my old horse Snip, and we headed up a steep trail toward the rim which loomed just above us on the western edge of the valley. We were running to the hills—his idea—and I loved it. He was riding my horse, and I was walking behind.

We made it maybe a half mile or so before I got tired of the climb and wanted to ride the horse and he wouldn't let me and I cried and we turned back in disarray. I can remember that rock-strewn hillside path quite exactly from almost fifty years ago, and how I came to hate his bullying. I was almost eight and he was something like ten and already deemed unschoolable, a poor boy with no father and a gray-faced mother who lived furtively inside that unpainted two-story crazy house where the doors wouldn't close and someone had nailed old coats over the broken windows. How he must have enjoyed his power over the spoiled little prick I was learning to be, with my horse and my little saddle.

My mother whipped me when I got home: for disobeying, for going down there in the first place, for wanting to run off to the hills, for letting him ride my horse, for letting him make me walk, for being a fool to his beguilements, for everything, I think, that frightened her. I remember that whipping and her strange fury. After that I knew she loved me as I had never known it before. And I learned my lesson: that crazy people are crazy, and they would steal from us and make *us* crazy if they could. But she wouldn't let them. We would never join them.

That fall, deep in the night, the crazy house burned down in a quick flare of irreversible excitement I watched from our front veranda. I suppose my mother was there with me. I remember those flames towering in the darkness for a few minutes, and in the morning there was a thin haze of smoke. Those dry warped planks had burned so perfectly that only the rough stonework foundation remained. The crazy people, the loutish boy and his broken mother, were simply gone. Not that anybody died. They were just gone, and we were all relieved. It was a working out, inevitable in its way, and best for everybody in the long run. Winter was coming. How would they have lived? You have to wonder where they went. It sounds like a fairy-tale story from this distance, with a moral. Such are the things we learn, and they are hard lessons to unlearn.

For a time I wondered if there were secrets nobody told me, thinking I was a child and wouldn't understand. Now I know there were many secrets they didn't even tell each other. We want to be good but it's hard to admit. Our generosities might be foolish, or just another form of selfishness. If we believe there is such a thing in the world as grace which accumulates with giving, aren't we in any long run simply serving ourselves, giving ourselves the gift of our own goodness? A true gift ought to be like water: it should flow to the sea and the clouds should form and the storms sweep inland until the rain has fallen on everyone. Such gifts can be thought of as the most central thing we seek to do in life as all day long we try to tell ourselves stories in which we have the luck to bring about some positive effect in the world.

I wish my mother and I had led Snip down through the sagebrush trail and given that old horse to the crazy people. I wish my father had hauled them a load of hay for the horse, and invited them up to our vast garden, to reap what they could, so they wouldn't have to steal vegetables in the night. I wish the crazy woman might have learned from us that it didn't matter so much if the world seemed unreal since it was at least decent, and that it is always a dream anyway, for everybody and not just her.

My mother was one of those venturesome women who are sure they are inhabiting history; they travel with a camera, preserving historic moments. I have hundreds of my mother's Brownie box-camera negatives, and I cherish them. A dozen or so are quite wonderful. The best one is best because it carries the heaviest weight of significances and secrets.

We think of our photographs as a way of preserving the instant, defeating mortality and serving as a trigger for our most precious memories. But they also work the other way. We see people we have cherished, who are changed or dead, and we are reminded of our own fragility; our photographs serve as doorways into the past and its stories, and as cautionary omens.

My favorite Warner Valley photograph is one my mother snapped on a cold day in the fall of 1943, down in the Thompson Field, during a lull in the branding. We lived a mile or so off camera. The tall man on the left is Ross Dollarhide. He was sixty-three at the time, and radiating the authority which derives from physical heedlessness. Ross Dollarhide was my main vaquero model in matters of grace and manliness. Those were important to a boy who had spent too much of his life being nursed.

Next to Dollarhide is Shorty McConnell, and next to Shorty is Hugh Cahill. I can't put a name to the big-hatted fellow at the end of the line. The man sharpening his knife, looking defeated and out of the picture-taking, is Roy Clark, who perhaps had reason to stand back. His father was Emmanuel Clark, who was cow-boss for Peter French in the early days of the country, and thus one of the kings amid our mountains. Roy had grown up with natural expectations, but it was rumored that he drank.

You have to wonder if Roy Clark thought he'd been tricked; somehow Dollarhide became the king of the make-believe in my boyhood, and in all our backlands empire, boss of all the cowboys for my grandfather. He drank and nobody cared; such considerations did not much apply to Ross Dollarhide. Ross took me on my first man-to-man trip to what we called "the desert" in 1941, just before the beginning of World War II, after my spring at Frémont School in Klamath Falls.

It was a long and serious day, in which I began to discover how to feel sheltered no matter how far removed from the gentleness of my mother and her household. We left before sunup in Dollarhide's black 1939 Ford V-8, and he returned me to home after midnight, a transformed boy who had traveled maybe three hundred miles of dusty, jolting wagon-track roads across the sagebrush and creosote flats, and down over the rimrocks, with a hard-handed legendary gentleman. A boy who had learned that such men never complained.

Some sixty miles out as the crow flies we reached our farthest remove from the irrigated enclave of Warner Valley at a place called Ackley Camp, an unpainted two-room line shack on a steep hillslope beside a good spring. The fine thing at Ackley was the view, a long vista over the sagebrush expanses of Hawk's Valley to the south and east. Skunk cabbage grew in the spring alongside the shack, and there was a watering trough and a woven willow horse corral. Dollarhide found black-and-red ants in the sugar. "Piss ants," he said, and he shook his head.

"Maybe they taste like piss," he said when I asked where they got the name. Despite the July heat, he built a fire in the wood stove, heated a can of stew, and fed me.

An old man I knew only as John the Swede held down the line camp at Ackley Mountain from May to early November, riding to look after MC Ranch cows and calves scattered across a territory the size of Rhode Island. It was a good sign that he was nowhere to be found; he was out horseback and working. We stacked a few crates of assorted canned goods on the kitchen floor, and Dollarhide left him a laboriously written note.

John the Swede was famous in our world because of his trips

to the Labor Day Rodeo in Lakeview. After four months at Ackley Camp, with no way to spend his money, the Swede would gear up with a full rig of new clothes, a barber shop bath and haircut and shave, and settle into a room in one of the half-dozen whorehouses out on the far side of the rodeo grounds, in a little village called Hollywood. After a week, the rodeo over, John would be ready to go back to the ringing silences on Ackley Mountain—fucked out, as they say, worn down by the booze and the talking, and broke.

You have to wonder if he was eager to return into a lifetime of dialogue with himself. Those men who went to the line camps seemed to cherish the isolation. "For a week or two," one of them told me, "you worry about what's going on in town, then you get so you can't remember town, and you sure as hell don't give a shit what they're doing."

While Dollarhide sat at the little kitchen table and composed his note with the thick stub of a carpenter's pencil, I nosed around and found a few words and even some phrases and verses inscribed into the softwood walls and doorjambs of the cabin. They were not just written, but inscribed, marked over and over with a heavy hand, cut into the grain of the wood, a few lines of rhyming poetry, some words from "The Strawberry Roan," the names of a woman, a man, and another woman, listed in a row like a mantra.

That's almost fifty years ago, and now I cannot recall any sense of those lost words and none of that verse. I would like to imagine that John the Swede spent some of his time at Ackley making up poems. I wish I could believe that the words he chose to inscribe into his walls would help me in my battle against my own isolation.

During the years of my young manhood after World War II, we developed the habit of listing the names of men traveling with the MC chuck wagon crew on the off-white oilcloth tacked to a kitchen wall in a camp in Guano Valley, an abandoned homestead called the Dougherty place. Each time the wagon visited, at least once during the early summer branding and again in the late fall, moving the cattle back home to winter on the meadows in Warner, we would print our names on the wall in order of rank, starting at the top with Ross Dollarhide, and ending with the cook and wrango boy. I was proud to be on those lists, and still am. I stopped to visit them anytime I was in the country.

But those lists are gone now. A highway was built across our deserts in the 1960s, close by the Dougherty place. Hitch-hiking travelers camped in those barren rooms, and added their names to the lists. Then, in the last half-dozen years, someone came in and stripped the place of all that oilcloth. I like to imagine some anthropologist has it now, preserved in a room with precisely controlled humidity. Which is ridiculous, I know. The paintings in the caves at Altamira and Lascaux are expressions of a dream, inhabited by animals, which was profoundly beautiful. Our lists of our own names on that oilcloth reflected the same instincts, our yearning to infuse our connections with significance, but they were beautiful only to us (and maybe to whoever took the oilcloth).

In late summer, just before the harvest, my father would take me and my brother and sister with him to his fields, and let us run trails through the oats. The crackling stalks were pale yellow and fragile.

Years later, when my life had gone different, when I was a man and those barley fields were mine to manage, and I was trying to make sense of my yearning to leave, I would walk out into my own crops as they came mature and stand studying the rims around the valley where I had thought I would always be at home, and I would lie down on my back and try to imagine that I was still a child and that my father was over at the edge of the field, talking irrigation with one of the hired men. All there was to see above me was the bright stalks and the spiked seed heads and the white sky.

Over something like three decades my family played out the entire melodrama of the nineteenth-century European novel. It was another real-life run of that masterplot which drives so many histories, domination of loved ones through a mix of power and affection; it is the story of ruling-class decadence that we fondle and love, that we reenact over and over, our worst bad habit and the prime source of our sadness about our society. We want to own everything, and we demand love. We are like children; we are spoiled and throw tantrums. Our wreckage is everywhere.

INTERLUDE

We tell stories to talk out the trouble in our lives, trouble otherwise so often unspeakable. It is one of our main ways of making our lives sensible. Trying to live without stories can make us crazy. They help us recognize what we believe to be most valuable in the world, and help us identify what we hold demonic.

Once I wrote a story called "Horses in Heaven." It turned on white horses running the hayfield meadows out below the house where I grew up on that high desert cattle ranch where my people lived like crown princes of irresponsibility, that lovely faraway horseback place where waterbirds came in the hundreds of thousands. See, I wanted to say, I love it still, although I have not lived there in many years.

The white horses had been spooked by the thunder and incandescence of a summer storm, and the story was about a frenzy of bloodiness after those horses ran themselves through a barbed wire fence. All that and love and death and some swimming. Quite a romance. There was a woman character who didn't want to live anymore, so she died, of something called "antidysthanasia," which was defined in my story as failure to take positive efforts to preserve life. There doesn't seem to be any such word in the real world.

An important part of my formal education can be thought of as starting with horses in the summer twilight of evenings in my early childhood. It maybe began the summer I turned four years old.

After he drove in from his fields and we were done with supper, my bare-armed father would lift me onto an old bay horse and lead me around our garden up behind the homesteader's orchard above the house. My mother was there, with my brother and baby sister; it was a moment. Serious men in our part of the world were horsemen. A boy who didn't have a right relationship with horses might end up at anything, like barbering or teaching, always fearful and ashamed in his secret heart.

It is possible to imagine paradise as a childhood among people who travel a turn of seasons while gathering their food, searching out various roots and waiting until the blossoms down along some drainage come ready into berries and fruit, once in a while killing an animal and praying to its spirit, giving thanks and eating the flesh. Think of your people, always on the move, always waking up in fresh country, and the way they would instruct you in the mysteries of a world so continuously new and strange.

Your mother would know the names of birds and you would echo those names. There would be a new thing to learn almost every day, the odor of sage entrapped in honey or some route down out of the mountains to the creek where the bear come to fish in the pools for spawning salmon.

Snaffle bit, concho, riata, remuda: those are names I was

learning, up there in the evening with my father, learning to sit a saddle. One of the things I recall as most valuable from my origins is the dry clean odor of horses, which is warm and fecund but not really nameable. It is the smell of those evenings along the high ditch above our garden where my father began teaching me what it is like to have a reciprocal relationship with an animal. And it was good for me, the attention we paid one another, the little boy and those horses.

My theories of human makeup tell me that it ought to be good for a child to start venturing out into life in a place and time where people still live in intimacy with the stink of animals. On the most simple-minded level I have to believe that the child who grows up surrounded by a sense of animals is likely to feel the world is really alive and vulnerable.

But mostly our knowledge of animals is a dim echo of real intimacy. We never really depend on the gift of their flesh for food; in Warner we killed waterbirds for sport, with shotguns, and we hunted deer and antelope, and killed them from a distance, with rifles. We were not people who sat still and studied animals in their wildness. The animals we knew were mostly domesticated and bred to perform a service, like pulling a plow, or running races, or fattening up to be eaten, or tamed and petted. Our relationships with such animals could be satisfying and driven by what seemed to be mutual affection, but their existence was dependent on our purposes.

My father was trying to give me something essential about the world as he knew it, which was horsemanship, but what I was learning, ultimately, was the art of keeping intimacy at some distance, and living with power. He taught me to enjoy it. I wish he had told me about the consequences, but likely he didn't know. I wish I had been able to talk about such things to my own children.

In the early years of World War II my father hired a man named Don Poncho to come to Warner Valley and work as a heavy-equipment operator. Don Poncho was from the Paiute band which lived around Winnemucca in northern Nevada. He brought his wife, whose name was Eva, and their children and stepchildren to live in a couple of floored, framed tent houses beside the row of poplars along the high ditch above the garden where on those childhood evenings I had learned to stay horseback and not fall off. The oldest of those stepchildren, a boy who became my closest friend, was named Vernon Wasson. He was much the quickest of us in any footrace.

This was about the same time I was given a little pinto horse named Dickie, half Morgan and half Shetland, thick in the neck and strong and stocking-footed and quicker than the working cowhorses in our remuda, a magical horse if magic in animals can be understood in terms of physical capabilities and good will and a discernible intelligence. There was the inevitable moment when my saddle turned, my foot hung up, and he could have dragged me to death or at least all the way home. But he didn't. Dickie stepped neatly around my helplessness and eyed me like a co-conspirator while I got myself disentangled and my hat back on my head and dusted my shirt so my mother would never know.

The summer I was eight, Dickie and Vernon and I were the world as it seemed destined to be; we were all that counted, together all day long, seeing everything, Vernon riding behind me on my little horse, children in a storybook who fished and found arrowheads and spied the hay-stacking crew from back in the willows. Then my father said there would be no more riding double, it was too hard on my little horse. I suppose there might have been some truth to it. Vernon walked, and sometimes he ran behind. Riding ahead, I was a perfect little imperialist. Then he sulked, and we went our ways.

Years later, out of high school in Winnemucca, so we heard, Vernon got a basketball ride to the University of Nevada in Reno. It was his main chance. But the summer before, feeding horses, he got stabbed in the eye with a pitchfork. At least that was the story we heard about why he was blind in one eye and lost out on his scholarship.

The last time I could have seen Vernon Wasson was in Lakeview during the Labor Day Rodeo, around 1960. "Your old friend Vernon Wasson," an Indian girl said, "he was looking for you, you could find him tomorrow. He's sick right now." Which meant he was drinking.

That was a friendship I had written off. Maybe I thought Vernon wanted to borrow money, I don't know, but I never tried to hunt him up. There was plenty of time, I must have thought, to turn all that stuff around and get it straight.

A few years later word came that Vernon Wasson had drunk himself to death, which may or may not have been true, but we believed it; it was one of those cautionary stories you hear while everybody shakes their heads about why doesn't anybody ever take any care. I was sad, for myself; I was finding certain failures could never be fixed.

What would a right relationship have been, all those years later, with Vernon Wasson? Knowing what I should have done was easy enough: I could have tried to help him. But I was unwilling to be bothered. Such basic incivility is a large part of antidysthanasia.

In graduate school at the University of Iowa, while America crunched along through the fall of 1968, I took what was called an "outside arts" course in filmmaking. The main thing I took away from that course is the idea that horses are emblematic of friendship.

My only film, lifetime, was a three-minute imitation of *Last Year at Marienbad* in which a blooded horse and a woman (my second wife) were revealed to be objects, things *owned* by the bourgeoisie. It was a story designed to reveal that I was as on to myself as any other grad student, self-reflexive and willing to swim anywhere in the sea of self-illumination which was our actual art.

"It's like humans are coded, genetically, to think horses are our friends," one of my friends said, in his graduate school manner. And I believed him. I still do. People are coded in lots of ways. They instinctively nuzzle their mother's breasts, love their children, and delight in what they take to be beauty. It's in the genes, like the wonder in your eyes.

My film was as foolish a beginning as such beginnings generally are; I was a serious boy of thirty-five at the time, deeply engaged in saving my life, yearning to mean things. But for a long time it did not seem that my life contained stories I could see as coherent, much less worth telling. My stories were mostly imitations about old men and wounded boys, reeking of sorrow and sad romance about the ways love is bound to fail, and could never have been enough anyway. I knew of nothing more valuable than self, which is another definition of antidysthanasia.

CHAPTER 4

THE PROMISE OF GENERATIONS

By the time I was eight, my grandfather had determined that my cousin Jack and I were plenty old enough to drive cows and begin our education in working-man horseback traditions and the demands of manhood.

On a day I recall as ecstatic, he bought my older cousin and me a couple of new saddles from the leather-smelling saddle-maker's shop in Lakeview. Mine was engraved and cost one hundred and twenty-five dollars; for many years it was the most expensive thing I owned, and I loved it as the surest part of what I was going to become. It was confirmed that I was going to be a horseman. All I had to do was stay tough enough.

The first real day of work set standards in rigor, at least in my mind, which were never really broken. In the early-morning darkness of a rainy day in April our cowhand crew headed out to gather dry cows (cows without calves, they were not giving milk) from the swamps of what was called the Big Beef Field.

And big it was, five miles square and half flooded by spring runoff, the sloughs deep enough to swim a horse.

Though my mother worried, my grandfather said something to the effect that nothing out there in the Big Beef Field was going to hurt that goddamned kid, which was supposed to make me proud. I was piss-your-pants scared. In that country of desert and small creeks we never learned to swim; it was one of our disabilities. But no need to worry, my grandfather said. Your horse can swim, just stick with your horse. And it was true.

Out there in the Big Beef Field my old horse named Moon was swimming half the time. The hides of those heavy-bellied cows ran slick with mud. Moon would pause as he labored through the sucking black mud in the tulebeds, I would grab the saddle horn with both hands, and he would go lunging out into the deep water which geysered up on all sides. I was frightened deep into mindlessness, and there was nothing to do but pretend I wasn't. I had discovered a terrible vulnerability in myself which I think of not as cowardliness but as an ability to imagine too much.

It is still there. I can't swim, and I am terrified of absolute heights, where a fall (or, more to the point, a leap) would be without recourse. This, of course, was an unfortunate fallibility in a boy with plans to become a horseback hero. And that first day wasn't really such a difficult day by buckaroo standards. By midafternoon we were turning our three thousand or so dry cows through the outside fence on the east side of Warner. My grandfather thought we ought to trail them along the beginnings of their fifty-mile walk to the deserts where they would summer. A couple of hours, he said.

But someone said something like "those kids got to be sent to the house, they're done in." My grandfather inspected us, saw it was true, and shook his head as if appalled by our sorry, worn-out childishness. Maybe it was there, at that moment, that I began learning my lesson. We were sent to the house, about ten miles, soaking wet and deeply chilled, and that terrifying day vanishes into a memory of riding on and on along a muddy levee bank into the deepening gloom of overcast twilight. And I made it. I was not absolutely doomed. I could make it.

That summer Jack and I started spending time on the desert, "out with the buckaroos." It was a couple of months on horseback, without any momma. It was our true beginning. How glorious it sounded. And it was, in many ways.

The first day lasted forever. It was our task to ride drag behind a couple of hundred meandering Hereford bulls as they were moved out of Warner toward the deserts to the east. Slowly, so slowly, we followed those loitering thick-skinned creatures up Greaser Canyon, their asses green with shit as they switched at flies, to a place called Hill Camp, where the four-horse chuck wagon was set up for the night. Before it was done I was almost sick with boredom. But I ought to have been sicker; I should have foreseen the future, and recognized a lifetime trailing livestock as a fate to be avoided at most any cost. It was twilight when we turned our horses loose to roll in the dust and run with the other seventy-some head in the remuda.

The cook, a woman named Lois Clair, clanged the dinner bell. The men laughed and joked in their impervious way. They were not used to the idea of a woman in camp. Kenny Clair, her young husband, the camp tender, usually known as the wrango boy, eyed them nervously. So did we, the owner's kids. We were facing our new lives, a couple of goddamned kids in a cow camp.

It is impossible to know what those men thought, and most

of them are dead now. But they treated us with rough decency, and saw us through. Those men were good to us, good enough. So was Lois Clair, a flint-hearted girl as I recall, but she would not let anybody pick on us, even though she made it clear she thought we'd been spoiled with too much mothering as it was. We ate our first meal in silence and then ran to climb the little cliffs behind the spring, where we found an old deteriorating box of dynamite nobody knew was there.

Within a couple of weeks I was refusing to wash. My lips and cheeks had sunburned, and I was accustomed to misery, sort of happy inside it, dirty and stubborn, gone somewhat feral. My schoolboy cheeks had cracked into deep scabbed-over furrows that bled and healed and broke open to heal again. Trying to remember those days I think I understand how children go naturally wild. It's like retreating into a cave, and finding the world is only a distant, unimportant noise. But maybe that's only the story I'm telling myself. I wonder if I know anything true about that child who wouldn't bathe, or even wash his crusted face, who stank. The men sent me down to the little creek below Sage Hen Springs with a bar of soap. Clean up, they said, holding up heavy scrub brushes, or we'll do it for you. I hated them.

The next summer, the straps on my new cowboy boots rubbed sores into the calves of my legs. The dim scars are there yet. Every day was a new day with my pain, saddle up, and nothing was real but pain; it was my life, everything else was unreal. It must never have occurred to me that I might ask someone for help, or simply take a pocketknife to the damned bootstraps. I don't think it was a misery I loved.

But it gave me excuses for fucking off. Along with stoic self-reliance I was learning the commonsense skills called "soldiering," those of insulating and protecting myself, lying back. Let some other damned fool do the volunteering. It was a lesson in goldbricking, and a sad lesson for a boy, which is taking a long time to unlearn.

"If I can stand this," I thought, "I can stand all they got, all my life." Children think such things. I lived with a secret pride, even in my shame; I loved myself, and knew I would never have to kill myself, ever, because I could stand the pain. I wonder if it's an understanding that will sustain me through the crippling miseries of old age.

One night we listened to news of Pearl Harbor on my father's big Hallicrafter ship-to-shore radio, our main connection to the outside world. The young woman who cooked for my mother went into hysterics. Positive that the Japanese were coming at any moment, she wanted to go to the bunkhouse and sleep with her husband. I remember thinking it would be all right, that somehow we'd fight them off.

When school recommenced in January, we would gather each morning around the upright piano and sing "Praise the Lord and Pass the Ammunition." I began to save pictures of fighting aircraft and trace them into my notebooks, icons of distant glory. But I have no memory of wanting to be a pilot; the romance of that was too distant to imagine.

A lot of able and well-connected young men were granted agricultural deferments. Raising food, the story went, was as important as shooting. Good help was scarce. Even so the young men who stayed home lived in a kind of hell. Old men called them cowards, and the label stuck when the war ended, and for decades afterward.

Toward midnight—at Adel Harvest Moon dances, say—some father whose son had enlisted in the navy and been shipped out to the possibility of death in the Pacific would flare into drunken prideful anger. The shouting and shoving and accusations would begin, and the good people who populate my memories of childhood would move to the parking lot where the fighting would start in the glare of headlights, men battering at each other, dust in little puffs around their feet, until one of them was defeated, slumped on his knees, spitting up a long spin of bloody drool.

Another part of our paradise was evaporating, but mostly it was still intact, and I think my father labored to keep it that way. During the war, wildlife biologists from the college in Corvallis told my father that sandhill cranes coming through Warner were rare and vanishing creatures, to be protected with the same intensity as the ring-necked Manchurian pheasants which had been imported from the hinterlands of China. The nests of these cranes, with their large speckled eggs, were to be regarded as absolutely precious. "No matter what," my father said, "we don't break those eggs."

My father was looking at me but talking to a tall gray-faced man named Clyde Bolton, who was stuck with a day of riding a drag made of heavy timbers across winter feedgrounds on the native meadows of the Thompson Field, breaking up cowshit before the irrigating started. This was so the chips wouldn't plug in the sickle bars of the John Deere mowing machines come summer and haying. Clyde was considered a pensioner since he had a damaged heart which kept him from heavy work, and he was married to Ada Bolton, the indispensable woman who cooked and kept house for us. Clyde milked the three or four cows my father kept, tended the chickens and the house garden, and took naps in the afternoon. He hadn't hired out for field work and he was unhappy.

But with help scarce during those years, there he was, take it or leave it. He had no real complaint. Riding the drag wouldn't hurt even a man with a damaged heart. Clyde had gone a little spoiled. That's what we used to say. Go easy on the hired help long enough, and they'll sour on you. A man, we would say, needs to get out in the open air and sweat a little, blow off the stink.

This was a Saturday morning in April after the winter frost had gone out of the ground, and I was a ten- or eleven-year-old boy learning the methodologies of field work. The nests my father talked about were hidden in the unmowed margins along the willow-lined sloughs in the yellow remnants of knee-high meadow grass from the summer before. "The ones the coons don't get," my father added.

I can see my father's gray-eyed good humor and his fedora hat pushed back on his forehead as he studied Clyde, and hear the ironic rasp in his voice. At that time he was more than ten years younger than I am now, a man come to the center of his world. I see Clyde Bolton hitching his suspenders and snorting over the idea of keeping an eye out for the nest of some damned bird. I can smell his disdain.

Going out with Clyde was as close to a formal initiation into field work as I ever got. There really wasn't much of anything for me to do, but it was important that I get used to the idea of working on days when I wasn't in school. It wouldn't hurt a damned bit. A boy should learn to help out where he can, and I knew it, so I was struggling to harness an old team of matched bay geldings, Dick and Dan, and my father and Clyde weren't helping because a boy would never make a man if you helped him all the time.

"You see what you think," my father said, and he spoke to Clyde seriously, man to man, ignoring me. All at once they were deeply serious, absorbed into what I understood as the secret lives of men. I studied them, watching for clues. My father acted like he was just beginning to detail Clyde's real assignment. You might have thought we faced a mindless day spent riding that drag behind a farting old team. But no, it seemed Clyde's real mission involved a survey of conditions. "Those swales are coming to pure swamp grass," my father said, sweeping his right arm to indicate all the meadow before us. "Drowning out." He went on to talk about the manure dams which spread the irrigation water. Clyde would have the day to study those dams and figure where they should be relocated.

It took me years to discover that my father wasn't much worried about swamp grass in the swales, and that Clyde Bolton knew he wasn't. This wasn't the point of their negotiations. What they both were concerned about was dignity: however fragile, an ultimate value.

"Your father was the damnedest son of a bitch," one of the old men at Warner told me. "He'd get you started on one thing, and make you think you were doing something important, and then he'd go off and you wouldn't see him for days, and pretty soon it was like you were working on your own place."

It was not until I was a man in the job my father perfected that I learned the sandhill cranes were not endangered at all. It didn't matter. Those birds were exotic and lovely as they danced their mating dances in our meadows, each circling the other with gawky, tall-bird elegance, balanced by their fluttering wings as they seized the impulse and loped across the meadows with their long necks extended to the sky and their beaks open to whatever ecstasy birds can know.

Sometimes I think my father was simply trying to teach me and everyone else on the property that certain vulnerabilities should be protected at whatever inconvenience. I wish there had been more instructions like this, and that they had been more explicit. Most of all I wish he had passed along some detailed notion of how to be boss.

Bossing people was a thing he seemed to do naturally. I wish he'd made clear to me the dangers of posturing in front of people who in some degree are dependent on your whims, posturing until you have got yourself deep into the fraud of replacing authenticity with mere distance. A man once told me to smoke cigars. "They see you peel that cellophane," he said, "and they know you don't live like they do."

By the late summer of 1943 or 1944, I'm not sure which, my grandfather decreed that Jack and I had turned out to be sort of useful when it came to herding cattle. In that we resembled actual horsemen.

A great adventure ensued. It turned on a herd of some fifteen hundred so-called Mexican steers my grandfather bought in the desert country of northern Mexico, and shipped to the Klamath Marsh for fattening. It was a major mistake. Those steers, it was said, were like dogs with horns. They were wild and various, unlike Herefords as they could be, all colors, splattered with patches of blue and red and mossy green, lean and quick, always prowling the fences, trying to escape into the jack pine forests, and impossible to fatten.

By late summer my grandfather had given up. I have no idea where he planned to ship them, maybe down to California for slaughter, maybe home to Mexico, but it was clearly time to get those steers off the Marsh. Gathering them, and getting them to the railroad siding and up the chutes into the railroad cars, as everybody knew, was going to prove a fearsome task. But I was eager for it. This was the real thing. I was going out into the world as one of the hands.

The Klamath Marsh was more than a couple of hundred miles away, connected to us by reasons of family and ownership but different, nearly sixteen thousand acres of meadow along the Williamson River in the center of the Klamath Indian Reservation, surrounded by timber. The Marsh was ruled by my aunt Vi and her husband, Bill Gouldin, a man legendary for his hard-assed candor and his belief that work would see you through. And Vi was her father's daughter, a lean woman who refused to sit home with the house and children when she could go horseback to fields and work cattle with the men. Who could blame her? Who could make it stick if they did? Vi was good-hearted and hard-working, frightening and hard-handed if you were used to a softer kind of woman. In her relationship with Bill Gouldin she was always the owner, with the ultimate power over yes or no in major decisions, and he was always the field boss, with his own absolute powers. Vi lived a long time after Bill Gouldin died, with a lot of money and power, and she understood both to be well earned. They were.

So the Klamath Marsh was another kingdom, where things were done in very particular workmanlike ways, and done over if they weren't right. There was no fooling around at the Klamath Marsh, not when Bill Gouldin had his eye on you. He was a ranch hand who had married the owner's daughter, and he was out to prove his worth every day. He was cut from my grandfather's cloth, his true son if there had been any justice.

A drought had dried the swamps on the Marsh until the peat ground opened in gapping cracks, four or five feet wide, ten feet down to water, and hundreds of yards long. So we were often traveling at a gallop after those absolutely untamed Mexican steers across meadows that were broken open like a checkerboard, the steers dodging ahead of us and our horses leaping the cracks. If your horse missed its footing and went down it would have been a terrible wreck, and you could have been killed. But nobody was hurt so far as I can remember. I recall the burnt smell of dry grass, the buzz of grasshoppers, drumming hooves on the hard sod, and the heedlessness of trusting everything to the surefootedness of your horse, running those meadows.

One bright morning, after those quick little many-colored steers were all corraled, we headed them down a long unfenced road through the jack pine timber to the railroad loading pens. If we lost them, they were gone to the unfenced forests of the Klamath Reservation, and to the high Cascades and anywhere. We took it very slow and easy, and almost made it. Then one of those railroad engineers pulled his steam whistle. Those steers came back at us, and went around us like we weren't there, in open stampede. I recall galloping through the scrub pine, trying to head them off, limbs whipping at my face and white pumice dust hanging in clouds around me. Some of those steers turned up two or three years later, at waterholes in the next county.

The spring of 1944, in the seventh grade, I went to Tamalpais School in San Rafael, California, with the children of ruling class South Americans. It was a horror show so far as I was concerned—boys showing each other how to jack off after lights out, no friends, no love, no nothing. It came to seem like a condition of life. The next year my mother bought a big house on Bryant Street in Palo Alto, and I went to Jordan Junior High. It was hard to understand why we had to live in California. We were told it was because of my sister's asthma, and that may have been partway true, but my father wasn't around very much during those years. So I have to think it also had to do with the state of my parents' marriage. Anyway, I eventually learned to ride a bicycle on the level streets with a pack of other boys, and play touch football in the park beside the perfect green where old men rolled bowls on the grass, and I liked it well enough.

So I was bitter that spring, 1945, when we moved again, to Red Bluff, in the upper end of the Sacramento Valley. My grandfather had bought sixteen thousand acres of grazing land in the rolling scrub-oak hills of the coast range near Paskenta, to the west. He'd be able to winter steers and heifers out there, ship them back to the Marsh in the spring, and send them on to the feedlot in the fall; my father could come down and look after them and spend some time with us. That was the idea, although I don't recall seeing much of him.

My bitterness was compounded when right away I came down with mumps, and they went down. There is nothing more pitiful than a horny thirteen-year-old kid who is bedbound in the spring of the year because his nuts are swollen to the size of softballs. He wants to lay hands on himself constantly, and doesn't dare, and occasionally does. My hormones, you could say with justice, were making me crazy. It was a rare moment I wasn't thinking about sex.

So it was a great relief when school was out and I could go back to the ranch and the desert, with all its exhausting diversions. I had learned to pay attention, and that boys should at least be handy. I had learned the necessity of work, for which I cannot say enough, and to keep my mouth shut while I tried to see things through. That summer I was almost healed into the horseback life forever.

One morning in early June, Jack and I went down to the round corral by the buckaroo camp in Warner Valley, shook out our ropes and caught our pinto horses in a boy's sure-handed casual way, saddled up, and rode some fifty miles out to join the chuck wagon crew at Catnip Reservoir. The day began with mosquitoes and our horses splashing through the irrigation water flowing across the uncut hayland meadows, and wild roses blooming on the fence lines. We crossed Beatty Bridge and the seventeen-mile outside dike my father had built around the east side of Warner, and were out into the smell of sage and alkali dust, heading for the long playa of Coleman Lake. You could feel the air turn dry as you left the swamplands.

What I felt as we rode those miles, up Coleman Canyon and across the scabby lava-rock benches on the old double-track wagon roads, and beyond the rim in Guano Valley, was more secure than schoolboy pride. The sun rose and the day heated up and my saddle creaked and my little pinto stank of sweat and warmth, and I kept feeling this was the right thing, natural and easy. This was my life. I was on to it at last; at least the boy's version.

By three in the afternoon we were eating roast beef sandwiches and a couple of sweet oranges in the shade of the chuck wagon tent on the grassy shelf above the big reservoir at Catnip. In the late afternoon, swimming down by the dam at the head of the reservoir, we were all in our skivvy shorts because the cook and another woman insisted on coming along. There were leeches clinging to our white legs when we waded ashore through the soft black knee-deep mud. When we tore them off, they left a bloody smear.

The men and women I knew in that childhood on the deserts seemed to understand that they had been granted fortunate lives. They gave everything to their luck, and understood that we cannot survive without such giving. We were what we could be. I sensed it at the time.

On the day after V-J Day, just a few days after I turned thirteen, I woke up to whiskey splattering onto my face. I was bedded down in my tarp and blankets on the splintery floor in the rambling old semiabandoned ranch house at the IXL Ranch in Guano Valley, in the sagebrush and lava-flow rimrock country along the Oregon-Nevada border. Through the broken uncurtained window I could see the sun just clearing the black terrace of rimrock to the east, but what I recall most vividly is Cecil Dixon standing over me as I came awake, drunk and grinning and sweating, taking a shot at pouring a long stream of whiskey into my open mouth because he loved me and wished me well, and wanted me to be a man.

Initiations, proper or not, stand in my mind as signs of community. Without them we can't hardly talk to one another in useful ways. That summer of 1945 was a time for gestures; the war was over. When the news about the bombs on Nagasaki and Hiroshima and then V-J Day came in on the radio, nobody knew what to do. Then somebody slapped the oilcloth and said it was time for a drink, and the tension broke, and all the men in my grandfather's cowhand haying crew at the IXL headed off in Ross Dollarhide's sharp-nosed black Ford V-8 for the little barroom desert town of Denio.

At least one thing loomed important about Denio: like the IXL, it was about a mile south of the line into Nevada. That meant all the border-town trafficking anybody wanted, booze and legalized gambling and local-option prostitution. In Denio those men could take a hot bath and hope to find women, and when the part with the women was over they could take another bath and buy beer by the case and any amount of whiskey. At least that's how they talked about what they were imagining.

They came back to the IXL that next morning with a carload of booze, up all night and having answered a need to stand heroic in the beginnings of a new age. That quick voyage can be thought of as an initiation in itself, of the kind those men grew practiced at working on themselves in their loneliness.

My moment with Cecil Dixon was as much a formal handshake into the possibilities of manhood as I ever got. A foolish little story, men without women, all those rituals. But for me it was a prime beginning, as useful in its way as anything I was likely to encounter in our disenfranchised end of the world. And as sexually simple-minded or complex as it might seem.

Cecil was saying, Welcome to the world where you get to be somebody like us, like me. It was an important thing for him to say, at least to a boy from the propertied classes, and he knew it. We knew about class if we didn't know about anything else. The men who worked horseback for the desert cow ranches in that country traveled from one chuck wagon to the next with their saddles and a sharp knife, clean clothes rolled inside their bedrolls and nothing much else beyond talent and independence and, once in a while, a harmonica.

As those men used to say, the company, whichever one you happened to be working for at the time, supplied everything but whiskey and sympathy: all the steak and milk gravy you could eat, lots of room to roll out your bed, a string of horses, soap. Old man Dollarhide used to bring us oranges by the crate. It sounds like a skewed remnant of the feudal system, and it was. Get on a drunk and get yourself fired and spend a week or so hanging around in town and then hire out to another cow camp where you would know somebody from some other outfit where you'd both worked some other season. And on around until you had worked for most of the big outfits two or three times, and you were an old hand, maybe crippled up a little and due some slack, looking for somewhere to settle.

That morning at the IXL Cecil Dixon was extending a rough-handed welcome across lines of money and governance. The free way it came conditioned my entire life thereafter. I thank Cecil Dixon, although he has been dead some years now.

You, he was saying, have earned your way. Not that I had, actually. Cecil was drunk and I was still the shit-for-brains kid whose grandfather owned the MC. But I wanted it to be true.

My people sent me to the desert as a child so I would learn how to work. My life since has been colored by what I got from four or five summers with those men. I was lucky to come of age knowing adults who in fundamental and good-humored ways were willing to spend their time and lives absolutely on the topic at hand, whether gentling horses or braiding rawhide ropes, with even-handed intelligence. They taught me to give what you have to your work and your life, even to use it up. I learned the story of Jesse Stahl, a black man who rode saddle broncs in the 1920s—the best there ever was, according to the men who saw him—and his death in the poorhouse in Great Falls, Montana. I still consider what it means to be the best in the world at what you do, with such rewards. You did what there was to do, that was the idea, without hurting your horses.

Dollarhide would have us out of bed by sunup, horseback and miles from camp by a quarter past five. Bellyaching was the major sin and I hate it still, with grievous impatience. If you don't like the way things are going, keep your mouth shut and quit. Somebody will give you a ride to town.

Childhood with those horsemen was partway populated by some sad-hearted and slick-skinned twits who amused themselves by picking on children. They treated their horses the same way. So fuck them; I wish my disdain could retrospectively wound them. But mostly these were good men who were kind to me. It's not hard to imagine why they took the time to treat a little boy with some consideration. By then it was obviously they would never manage to have a home, and I was their boy for a summer, even if I was the owner's son. Sometimes loneliness is only loneliness.

My mother thanked them for their kindness, but I never knew what to say when I saw them years later, in Lakeview at the rodeo, dressed up in their town clothes and a little drunk, as I was, in my college boy way, and we all seemed to be other people altogether. Now I am going to take this chance to praise them, not that it will do them any good. They were mostly young men, and yet many of them have been dead a long while, vastly before their time. Cowherding is a way of life which, if you aren't selfish enough to stay defensive, can seep into the cracks and kill you. Generosity can come to equal weakness. That is a lesson which can drive us away from one another, but with them it didn't. If I was to be happy, they taught me, I had to love my fate and embrace my future, which was going to be a horseback ranchland life if I had any sense, and live through it with some vigor, entertained and delighted. For a long time, as a boy and young man, I never doubted it. I believed, and I tried, and it almost worked. But 1945 was the end of cowboying for me. I was coming fourteen the next summer, and I was never going to be a great hand with horses. Field work was six bucks a day in the late 1940s, buckarooing was four. I opted to stay in the valley and work in the haying. I drove a hay rake and set nets for the stacking crew. I could take a shower every night, with fresh towels, and there were girls nearby, not that I was game to go after them. I could always go back to the desert some other year. But I never did.

That fall, back in Red Bluff, a freshman in high school, I learned to look into a mirror and smile. I smiled at everybody because I wanted to be popular. My cousin Sue, Vi's daughter, was a couple of years older than I was and lived with us that year. She was good-looking and popular, a cheerleader; and she was kind to me, a thumb-sucker if there ever was one. I had a crush on her in a fervid schoolboy kind of way that kept my mind busy. And I played football on the street in front of our house on Saturday morning, and learned the words to a lot of songs, not that I had the courage to ask anybody to dance. But I would, next year, Sue assured me, when I was a sophomore, and everybody knew it. In the grip of such expectations it was a perfect 1940s small-town American school year, a real movie, as they say.

In the late fall there was an exciting run of days when my grandfather and my father and Vi and Bill Gouldin and some of the cowhands from Warner showed up to off-load a herd of steers and heifers from railroad cars. It took all one long day, from first light until dark, to drive them the seventeen or so miles to the grazing land we owned in the hills to the west. My mother got me out of bed at three in the morning. I drank coffee with the men, and I was happy. None of those dance-masters at Red Bluff Union High School would ever make a hand at this kind of work.

In the late spring we gathered the cattle off the scrub-oak hills, and that was not so festive. It rained and the hills were muddy and slick and we were wet and cold. My brother, Pat, still a boy and never given much of a chance with horses, got scraped off on a tree limb. He rode the rest of the day, saying he was hurt, and eventually he cried. My grandfather was furious and called him a baby. Turned out Pat's arm was broken. That was the first time I truly listened when people said my grandfather was an asshole.

During those mysterious years at the end of World War II my father unexpectedly made a lot of money farming grain off the plowgrounds of Warner Valley. Money he didn't have to split with my grandfather or anybody, a fact which in the end caused heavy grief in our family. And he proved, as my mother once said, to be ahead of his time in finding ways to spend it.

For a few years during the war, as the catskinners brought more and more of the swampland under drainage and the plow, economics in my family depended more and more on the spectacular profits from my father's farming operations. And my father was running with his luck, blowing some money; there were movie people, an airplane, even a couple of racehorses. But mostly, even ahead of the game, in my family we worked.

My father bought two more D-7 Caterpillar tractors, and four John Deere combines with sixteen-foot headers, and kept them busy. The seventeen-mile diversion canal was finished; inside the canal he built a network of drainage ditches and redwood headgates. The shallow lakes were pumped dry, huge fields were ditched off, seven hundred and fifty acres in Huston Swamp, eight hundred acres in Dodson Lake. The headgates were opened when the spring runoff waters came, and those fields were flooded and pumped dry again. We were reinventing the land and the water-flow patterns of the valley on a model copied from industry, and irrevocably altering the ecology of everything, including our own lives; moving into the monied technology which is agribusiness.

In the spring of 1946, with the war ended, came a simple and enormous change. We started putting up the loose hay on our fifteen or so thousand acres of wild meadow with tractors. Our work teams were sold off for chicken feed. A splendor and attachment to seven or eight thousand years of human experimentation and tradition went from our lives with those horses.

I recall the dust and the slow drumlike clomping of their hooves on the dry sod of the late July fields as they snorted and trotted amiably toward the hay-camp corrals before sunup. After we sold them the harness hung on pegs in the barns, and rotted.

In the haying we had traditionally employed crews of nearly a hundred men through the summer months—some coming, some working, some going—thirty mowing machines and twenty dump rakes, and maybe two hundred head of workhorses. Two stacking crews followed the mowing after a week or so of letting the hay cure, dragging loads of hay up over the beaver slides into hundred-ton stacks, a hundred-ton stack every half day through July and some of August when they were up to speed.

As these crews and their cooks moved around the valley from hay camp to hay camp, it was a place filled with human life. You could look out over Warner Valley in the morning and see the strings of dust rising to clean sky over those hay-camp corrals, stirred up by the circling horses as the crews caught their teams. You could think this was the right dream, and I still do, before I stop myself: ourselves as we were supposed to be before everything went to tractors.

All the business dealings inside our family were contractual, but my grandfather felt tricked anyway. He had got control of the property in Warner Valley by putting up everything he had worked for all his life, and now my father was defying him, making huge money and a lot of it was not going back into the property. Racehorses and airplanes. My grandfather could not endure such things, and eventually became obsessed with ideas of revenge against his own son, doing my father out of his turn as head of the family. And it worked. Soon there was no family. To his death my father spoke of his father with contempt.

One evening, after we'd been fishing down on Twenty Mile Creek, I rode home through the twilight with Henry Nicol in his old gray coupe. Maybe I was used to drunks, I don't know, but I do know I was surprised when he ran off the winding gravel road, out through the shallow barrow pit, and into the sagebrush. We sat there awhile. Nick studied the lights on the dashboard, and looked over to me. "Son of a bitch," he said, in that heavy voice. Then we worked around and got the coupe back on the road, and when we got home I never said anything and neither did Nick. But it wasn't long before my mother said Nick had offered to teach me how to drive, what did I think about that?

What I remember is slowly progressing up and down the old country road across Warner Valley, Nick with a bottle of beer in his hand, sipping along while we started over and over again, me grinding the gears in his old pickup, Nick seeing me through my troubles. For me it was a gift. In such dreams we learn to love what we can foresee of life, and to value ourselves.

After that year in Red Bluff, my mother bought a big house up on Third Street in Klamath Falls, just a couple of blocks uphill from the Elks Club where my father did his main drinking and card playing. My mother bought a pool table and put it in the basement, with the idea that now I could have friends over to the house. Maybe my father would play with us. And he did show up a few times, to demonstrate some masse shots. But the basic idea was a joke: Oscar Kittredge in the basement, shooting pool with some kids, when the Elks Club was just down the street.

Although he kept a stranger's hours, we saw more of him. He studied us with perplexity, and maybe even tried to make us happy. But he had decided, I think, that his children were never going to amount to much, and he wasn't inclined to waste time on failures.

During my last years in high school my father would hire my schoolboy friends to work in the hayfields at Warner. He understood that they were relief for my isolation, as his friends were relief for his. A boy named Jim Carter came the summer we were sixteen. Handsome and blond, the monied only son of a dentist, Jim seemed born to graceful ways with certain girls, and to carelessness. I think he pitied me a little because I had no way with girls at all. For God's sake, he seemed to think, they're so fucking easy, are you helpless? We were a preening, hair-combing batch of boys, devoted to deep suntans and the muscular look of our hard forearms, youth in our prime and as simple and sweet and as ignorant, it seems, as toads in a pond.

On the weekend of the Fourth of July of 1949 we got drunk and shot skyrockets through the second-floor windows of a brick whorehouse in Klamath Falls called the Palm Hotel. Then all of my friends gathered at our house on Third Street while I took a screwdriver to the hinges on the locked cabinet where my father kept his booze. I spent the next couple of days being hauled around half naked and insensible and puking in the trunk of Jimmy Carter's car; nearly died, close as I can make out, of alcohol poisoning. Jim Carter has been dead for thirty years. He hit a tree along the highway on a ski trip to Mount Shasta, where the skiing has always been lousy.

My father had made powerful friends, heavy-bellied midlife men like Pat McCarran, a United States senator from Nevada and a bad politician if there ever was one (examine the nature of his dealings with the Paiute Reservation at Pyramid Lake). There was a man named Cord who drove one of the famous automobiles he'd named after himself up to us across the dirt-road deserts from Reno, and movie people, in particular a glossy-haired singing actor named Dennis Morgan. He was in a lot of sheik movies, and seen as developing into a latter-day Valentino, a laughable idea if you've seen any of his films. And Dennis Morgan's friends, the minor actors, the lawyer and the agent, the publicist and the casting director.

Owing to what was no doubt some confusion about hunting seasons, one time the Hollywood bunch showed up at my father's house in midsummer with their coolers stocked. The actors instigated a macho Sunday morning football game with the suntanned boys on the front lawn, and they cheated. They tripped us, they pushed, they apologized, and then did it again. They beat us and taught us a sullen lesson. Your father's fanciest friends can turn out to be jerks. Even your father can laugh it off.

But not always. During those years, in cahoots with a man named Marshall Cornett, who was president of the Oregon State Senate, my father bought a Beechcraft Bonanza, an airplane which seated four people and was considered to be pretty full-scale and quite a decent piece of machinery; it was the sort of thing rich men owned. Neither my father nor Marshall Cornett could fly, so they hired the piloting done, mostly by an experienced man named Cliff Hogue. It was the safe thing. Cliff Hogue would land down on the meadows of the Thompson Field, in front of our house, and spend the morning taking us kids for rides, dipping the wings and giving us our little frights. He seemed to enjoy it himself. It was the best of worlds, ours as a plaything.

In late October 1947 a trip to the waterbird hunting in Warner got organized. There was Earl Snell, governor of Oregon, and the secretary of state, Robert Farrell, and Marshall

Cornett, and Cliff Hogue, the pilot. It was October 27, a stormy day, and they flew anyway, to Klamath Falls, where they stopped for dinner at Cornett's home. Then they flew on into oncoming darkness and spitting snow, heading for Warner. My father was waiting eight or ten air miles east of the valley, at Coleman Lake, an alkaline playa where the Beechcraft could land. He waited through the stony gray light of evening and into darkness, and they did not come, and they never came.

Their remains were found the next morning, on Bly Mountain. The Beechcraft was destroyed. It had pancaked in and skidded under the lower limbs of a huge juniper, killing them instantly so far as anyone could tell. A man like my father, while he waited, before he decided there was some terrible trouble and came in to call the state police, he would think. As the publicity started and went on, everybody would wonder—you would hear things if you listened a little—if Oscar Kittredge hadn't got beyond himself getting mixed up with that damned airplane in the first place and now this is the price everybody has to pay, the governor dead and all of them, the state government and the Republican party in ruins.

You would know the people who said such things were small-minded shits, but if you were a boy at the time you would hear them anyway, murmuring as people do in any community. It was a time when I averted my eyes instead of watching while my father got his lesson. I could have learned something about the uses of compassion, but I didn't. I wasn't ready for cautionary tales.

On long evenings while my friends and I worked out those summers as hayfield boys, we would get our lightweight .22-caliber rifles and let the windshield down on an old red war-surplus jeep, and head out a dozen or so miles to the playa at Coleman Lake for the jackrabbit hunting. Which was slaughtering, really—and just the thing, since we were young and seething.

The white alkaline bed of the dry lake was maybe five miles across and smooth as a raceway. Around the edges, coming out of the low brush into the coolness of the evening, thousands of long-eared jackrabbits roamed in enormous clusters. It was a legendary population explosion and maybe evidence of profound ecological imbalance. We thought of it as combat; my .22 was equipped with a rapid-fire device, and I sprayed bullets with the true coldhearted enthusiasm of a soldiering schoolboy, thrilled by the sound of it and my ability to send jackrabbits twitching and dying into the dust.

One evening I ran out of shells, and took to clubbing the frantic rabbits with the butt of my .22 as we drove, every so often hitting one, sending it cartwheeling. It was cheaper than shooting, and just as gratifying. Until I struck the ground and shattered the hardwood stock on the rifle. I felt like an asshole, and pitied myself.

Although we kept a so-called kill count that ran up into the dozens, nobody collected those rabbits, and nobody knew how many were actually killed, how many wounded. They were rumored to have a disease of the blood, so nobody wanted to touch them. I still feel the excitement of those hapless boys. We didn't know anything.

It was a Monday, and Charlie Klatzenbaugh swore he thought it was Sunday. "I woke up way out in the brush," he said, speaking carefully, as he always did, talking about the little hillslope north of the Adel Community Hall, and the bottle of whiskey about half full, the morning light glinting through it, there beside him, in the sagebrush.

Charlie thought it was Sunday and a day off from haying, so he had a drink to ease his troubles, and then another, and then he walked, packing the bottle, down the road toward the ranch, a mile or so, and he was surprised as hell to see us all going out to work. It turned out to be Monday; he'd skipped a day resting there on that hill north of the dance hall.

But he was game, so he tried. Charlie climbed on the back of the truck and rode out to the fields, running his John Deere mow tractor around in some circles with the cutter bar whirring, and then he tumbled off with the clutch still kicked in, which meant somebody had to catch the tractor, climb on, and shut it down. Catching that John Deere was a somewhat risky business in itself, but it was nothing compared to falling off with the cutter bar whirring away, quick and deadly. Charlie just missed falling into it, and he knew it as soon as he sat up grinning like a man who had tricked death—and watched the field boss run down his tractor.

Later on, after he'd been fired and I'd been appointed to haul him to the house and the bookkeeper had given him his check, Charlie just fell out on the lawn like he intended to lie there forever. My grandfather came to stare down at him. "My boy," he said to a man who must have been fifty years old, "I pity you." Charlie laughed. At fifteen I knew what was funny, and I laughed with him.

In our part of the world most men of substance and property (at least those who were not Catholic, like the mostly County Cork Irish who shared Warner Valley with us) were members of the Masonic Shrine. My father spent some years working his way up in the hierarchy. After a while it was understood that he would spend the last week of each year in San Francisco, helping to get the pump primed for the Shriners' East-West Game on New Year's Day, big doings in those times, the late 1940s. He took the family with him, all of us, to live for a week in the old Palace Hotel on lower Market Street.

Which didn't mean much to me until the winter I was sixteen, the year my father was actually Potentate of the Shriners in eastern Oregon. I found that I could go to him for money when he was drinking with his friends, and he would always haul out another twenty, even if I had bummed him only an hour or so before. I don't know what he thought I was buying, and most likely he was paying me no attention at all. Soon I had quite a roll, like a hundred and fifty bucks, which was some real money for a sixteen-year-old in 1948. Where could a country boy spend so much, except on whores?

Somewhere I'd heard that drivers for the Veteran's Taxicab Company could find you a whore. I was a high school kid who had been to the whorehouses, Hollywood in Lakeview, and the Palm Hotel and Irene's and the Iron Door in Klamath Falls. So what the hell. Whores were not an answer to some physical need. They were pure adventure.

I stepped out in front of the Palace Hotel like an experienced dude and hailed a Veteran's cab. There is no telling what the driver thought, but he took pity and delivered me to some down-at-the-heels uptown hotel, and even told me how to conduct myself once I was inside. Just tell them single room, he said, cheap. Tell them you want a half hour. Otherwise, kid like you, they'll sell you some suite. So I marched in and got me a room for about thirteen dollars. They told me to wait and the girl would be along. There was no chair, so I sat on the bed.

It was an hour before the door rattled and flew open. The woman who confronted me was maybe thirty, blond and heavyset in a Joan Blondell sort of way. She looked to be absolutely stunned, then pissed off. "Fucking kid," she said, and she turned and marched out of the room, slamming the door behind her, never to return.

Finally I got my nerve up, and I thought fuck you, fuck this and everything around here, and fuck my thirteen-dollar room and Veteran's taxi ride. I walked out, leaving the door open behind me, and made my way down the long brown hallway toward the rear of the building where I wouldn't have to face the grinning jerk at the desk who sold me the room, who no doubt had heard all about this latest disgrace. I made my way down a narrow stairwell, slipped out the fire exit, and walked the nighttime streets, sipping the wine of disenchantment, thinking things would always be like this, life being the lonesome work it was.

Walking home to the Palace from my whorehouse hotel, I at least thought I saw the whole turtle, actual and live: a bright array of city lights, a line of infidelities. Heartaches by the number. Hello, window. Is that a teardrop in your eye?

But only a night or so later, driven by my mother's tongue and a foolish promise, my father found himself insisting he and I go out into the night, specifically to one of the places where I'd been spending my time and his money. This, I figured, was my mother's way of getting someone to check on my doings. There's no guessing what she might have suspected, though I doubt that she was worried that whores were snorting at her boy. But I grasped at the chance to educate my father into the realities of the city after sundown, the heat of night life. I would take him to see my one-armed trumpeter, a secret I could show him the way he showed me his money. An honest trade and a little showing off.

All this is difficult to discuss with any assurance because I don't really credit the good taste I showed so many years ago. How can I have discovered Wingy Manone? He was one of the fine jazz trumpeters, not an immortal like Roy Eldridge, but one of the brilliant players—reputed to be the first man to run the basic lick which became "In the Mood," and that's real history. How can I have known such things and then lost them? How can I have stumbled across them in the first place?

In any event, with some pride I led my father out to one of my advanced-thinking jazz haunts. We entered a narrow room off lower Market, not far from our hotel, gleaming with dull chrome and polished hardwood in my memory, where I had been listening to a little back-of-the-bar group led by my Wingy Manone. I loved the notion of black people and their music. It was more than music, I thought, in my good-hearted way; it was elemental, and part of the energy driving the whirl of things.

We sat at the bar, up close to where the band was perched on a little platform just behind the bartenders, almost within reach. All of us, performers and audience, were in a kind of sweaty intimacy, and it must have seemed a little much for my father. Before long he bought a round for the house, a terrific gesture and an attention-getting sort of move, maybe fifty bucks in 1948 dollars. The bartenders went right to work, mixing and pouring. Everybody was impressed, even me.

"What'll you have?" Wingy Manone asked, meaning music.

"About ten minutes of silence," my father said.

Wingy Manone just smiled big as life and lifted the drink my father had bought. "You bought it," he said, and he looked to be truly pleased.

There was a graceful little intermission while my father chatted with Wingy Manone and everybody talked and downed the drinks my father had bought, before Wingy tipped my fa-

ther a wink and started playing a few gentle notes. So maybe
somebody did explain my options to me, maybe I should have
got it loud and clear. Wingy Manone and my father, dealing
their lives in such confident ways—they were acting out the
options: be somebody or don't, but understand that nobody
owes you a good time or decency or money or anything. But
like a baby boy, for a long time in my life, I thought I was
owed, thinking poor me—so happy, once. It is a thought I've
often had.

The next summer that legendary worker Bill Gouldin fell off a
haystack at the Klamath Marsh and hurt his back. At least that
was the story. Probably he was already suffering the heart trouble that eventually killed him. I was asked back to the Klamath
Marsh as a man, to take his place pitching hay on the stack,
the hardest day-after-day physical labor there was on those
ranches. A big soft kid, Bill Gouldin said; might as well see if
he can work. I took it as a sure sign of promotion into actual
manhood.

For a while it was a nightmare. I was exhausted by noon and
mindless by quitting time. I learned to tie my pants legs with
twine to keep the chaff from working up inside them. I ate
everything I could get my hands on and lost twenty pounds in
twenty days. Right after dinner, by sundown, I was in bed, and
I ached everywhere when I crawled out in the morning.

I worked with Glenn Tingley, who had been married to my
cousin Sue for a couple of years. I wouldn't have lasted three
days without him. Glenn was older than I was, and hardened
from working a couple of years with Bill Gouldin. One of these
days, he told me, he was going to go back to college and become a coach. That was our great question: Stay on the ranch,

or go out into the world? Glenn stayed until the company was sold. He carried me for a couple of weeks, until I began to toughen up. "Can't quit," he'd say. "What would Grandpa think?"

Glenn would grin and we'd suck at hard candy and go back at the brutal work. Then one day there was a breeze and a break in the work, and we were up there on the stack, maybe thirty feet off the ground—it was almost noon and I wasn't even tired and we were looking down on everybody, leaning on our pitchforks and kings of the mountain.

Toward the end of that season, Henry Nicol died of heart trouble. He was one of the people who'd been good to me, and I went through his funeral as an enactment, without grief, unable to know what grief would be, searching to find out, deep into a young man's drunk at the wake, ranting for the benefit of handsome older women. My mother didn't say anything as I sat on the back steps and wept to the moon and then cursed all creation while the sun rose. Manhood had turned out to be a lonesome place where I didn't much want to live.

"I thought you had gone crazy," my mother told me lately, smiling, in her eighties, confined to bed. She doesn't seem to think any sort of human conduct is crazy anymore.

There is a man I see when I go back to southeastern Oregon, a good man who has earned the respect of his people. He is a man I fear, gone horseback to the desert each summer, and to Korea instead of college. He was a near miss for me.

That man is home, where I could have been. I was born to it, but I left. As a consequence I carry a little hollow spot inside me. Part of me despises that man—he settled so easily, in such an unquestioning way—while in another part I despise myself for having given away that possibility. I am tempted, because I didn't see it through, to think of myself as cowardly.

I have to keep telling myself, when I go visiting back in Lakeview or Burns, as I sit over an early breakfast in some highway café, eyeing some man I might have been, that it's all right, I get to be what I want. It's a free country. But then . . .

CHAPTER 5

THE BEAUTIFUL HOUSE

They would die in separate lives and far from one
another, despite oaths exchanged when they
were young.

—RAYMOND CARVER,
"The Offending Eel"

For a long time I wanted to be a football player. Not a star—
I never had the natural talent for that, and I'd made my
mind up to live with it—but a blocking back, some kind
of finely trained true-hearted journeyman. And then a coach, a
high school coach, in a little town in the interior. It would be
a respectable career, a life.

This was a dream of possibility I discovered when I first got
myself to go out for sports, the fall of my freshman year at Red
Bluff Union High School in the Sacramento Valley, and I went
on with it in Klamath Falls, and at Menlo School, down in
California. I bought books about football, and collected plays
on three-by-five cards; I believed in football religiously, just as
I have come to believe in other cures for my life.

But I was slow-footed, and never tough enough. My freshman year at Oregon State I yearned to be an athlete, and I was
lucky enough to live in a fraternity house full of them. For years

I knew people playing in the National Football League, but I was soon convinced to give up my own ambitions. That first fall in Corvallis I played on the freshman football team. We used to scrimmage with the varsity, helping them prepare for their next game. Once in a while I would play across the line from a giant quick-handed Hawaiian fellow named Herman Clark, who later played nose guard for the Chicago Bears. Herman would knock me backward about ten yards in a good-natured sort of way, and then laugh. It was easy for him, and it was clear I couldn't really play.

So I didn't go out for spring practice, and spent the spring of 1950 learning to smoke cigarettes. I lived with some older men—ex-GIs from California who'd served in the war—in a basement room in the fraternity house, and I went back to loving jazz. We would play *Jazz at the Philharmonic* records (Flip Phillips on "Perdido") deep into the night, and we would have taken any drugs we could get if we'd been given the chance.

I was intent on being someone who didn't care if the sun came up. I had grown up to look like a man but was still a child, my life one imitation after another. I was becoming a collector—books, buttery-orange little 45-rpm records—instead of reinventing myself.

Girls came to me like creatures from some other continent. They spoke the same language, but who could know what they meant?

The first girl who was ever good to me, I used to claim, was the one I married; and while it was a stupid remark, the whole matter was no joke to a boy as thickheaded as me. For a long time I had been one of those young men doomed never to have any luck with girls, which worked out to mean futureless: no football, no girls, nothing but cigarettes and the cheap company of your peers.

And then in some miracle—after a snowball fight as I recall—we kissed, I asked her out, she said sure in some way like that, and everything changed. It must have been January 1951. By spring I had given her my fraternity pin and we were an official couple with our twenty-year-old friends, which meant we held hands as we walked the bucolic lawns across the Oregon State campus, and we always went places together, even to the coast for a weekend. It was certified young love, and I was no longer the outcast boy.

We ran in a pack with others. That spring we all took a widely known gut course in art interpretation; I was good at identifying slides of famous paintings, and bright young women sought out my conversations. Abruptly I was someone else. It was the most vivid springtime of my life, everything in bloom and all of it colored by the sadness of oncoming separation from my true love and my new self. In June I would have to go home to the hayfields in Warner Valley.

When I drove away, I was too witless or too deeply confirmed in a pattern of ranch-boy powerlessness to think of not going. I wept, determined to be every bit as inconsolable as that child with his polio, screaming as his mother left his long-ago hospital room. I promised to write every day, and I did; she said she would too, and she did. She was so beautiful. Such was my insecurity that I counted the letters. Each night I came in from haying, spoke to no one, and settled in for a mournful session of letter writing. Soon I would be weeping. I seized any excuse to see her. I said my family wanted to meet her.

So Janet came to visit. After all, we were pinned, which could mean engaged. All I recall is driving her to Coleman Lake in an old pickup one hot afternoon when I was drunk on beer. It is hard to exaggerate the vastness of that barren playa.

She was a girl from town. I told her about killing jackrabbits, and that I wanted to make love to her, there in the seat of that old GMC pickup truck while the white dust blew. She refused, as firmly and sweetly as could be hoped; only she can know what she thought. She could have broken it off, but something turned. She said it was all right. I took her patience as a promise.

What we thought we were going to do, in our beginning, was get everything right and never make any mistakes, so long as we lived. I remember the ways we were going to be generous. And the ways we failed and found reasons to ignore the possibility of absolutely giving ourselves away. I wish I could say it was because we didn't try. But it wasn't anything so simple.

We tried hard at being good to each other, and we thought that meant we were being good to the world, and for a long time it seemed to be working. We thought ours was the special case, ours the connection that would never fail. By now we've been divorced for twenty-five years. What did we ask of each other that was too much? How did our inabilities manifest themselves? Maybe we were too careful, and tried to be too good.

In December 1951, when we were nineteen, Janet and I were quite formally married, after religious instruction, in a ceremony that took place in a fine hardwood Presbyterian church in Corvallis. She in a long white dress, and I in a white, college-boy dinner jacket. We spent our first night in the Eugene Hotel, and the next day we visited the Sea Lion Caves. We were children—strangers, really—but we were decent children, and we tried to accommodate each other.

Here it began. She worked Christmas vacation checking groceries for Safeway; I lay on the couch in our students' apartment and read Henry Steele Commager's two-volume *History of the United States* from cover to cover. This was all strange ground. I was a married man and was supposed to be looking for work, but I'd never read a book like that, so many pages and so serious and filled with things I didn't know. I started making lists of Civil War battles; I couldn't stop.

That was my first encounter with my own ignorance, and the realization that my education had been appalling. I knew nothing of the world. I didn't really know much about ranching, or about the farming in which my father had made his reputation. From my first quarter at Oregon State there were professors of agriculture who would lecture the class about my father's avant-garde irrigation practices, and turn to me for answers to their questions. I didn't know what they were talking about.

And now I could not stop my reading; this was an end to such ignorance. I was a married man, I should've had a job and felt some guilt that I didn't, but I went on reading anyway. And there began one of the retreats of my life, which I have to respect as a move, however neurotic, toward salvation. As illiterate boys will, I came to books, and learned to value ideas beyond anything actual which might be happening right at the time. I reread *Moby-Dick* and *Walden* and the Cornford translation of the *Republic* three times each during my senior year at Oregon State, as if they had to be memorized. As the books piled up around my life like barricades, I turned away from my friends and their athletics, and became the worst sort of schoolboy pedant.

The next summer we went back for a family gathering at

Odell Lake on the Fourth of July, several days of big fish and young love. The main players in a drama centered on deep trolling for lake trout were my father, my sister, and Janet, the big winner. My father was the guide, Janet caught two huge trout and got her picture in the *Oregonian*, and my sister sulked. Roberta was about fourteen, and had grown into a stocky, brassy, good-guy girl, my father's favorite, his utterly forgivable baby. Roberta has always been game, and a player all the way, but she wasn't used to being outfished by a girl from town. She hated it, and it showed, and everybody made it worse because nobody paid much attention to her posturing. We were busy tending other fires.

Janet's sister, Maryann, was what we in those days called a looker, and she had come to the lake with us. She and my cousin Jack locked on each other. We took long morning boat rides, and then in the late afternoon, Jack and Maryann would wander away. We were young and in love and we trusted one another. We would be friends forever, a sure thing.

Later that summer we all took a trip to Reno, and Jack and Maryann were married in the courthouse by a judge who kept hunting dogs in his chambers. The alliances forged that slow summer echoed in our lives through the next couple of decades, until we split apart, scarcely ever to see one another again, probably unto death.

The immediate years were like time out from real life. Janet gave up her college and checked groceries; I took money from my parents and worked at occasional jobs for the agricultural research agencies connected to Oregon State, counting beets in a row, things like that. But books were my obsession and sickness. I had discovered a separate kingdom where nobody lived but me, a place made of ideas.

The idea of writing was something I came to about the same

time. Maybe all of it started with my incapacities and my failures at what were thought to be mannish things. Maybe I wanted a world in which I was the one who made things up.

To say it was power I was after might be too easy and clever. Or maybe we could blame it on poor lost Hemingway. It was while reading him that I first sensed storytelling as a useful thing to do, which, in light of his misadventures, makes my conjecture about power and masculine failures sound more plausible. The door to all this had first been eased open for me through the efforts of a teacher my junior year at Klamath Union High School. That sainted man (I cannot recall his name) drove a crowd of us schoolboy semijocks to memorize a little James Whitcomb Riley and Emerson and Whitman, and he tricked us into liking it. I came away thinking certain parts of poetry were among the things I admired, almost as much as the music of Hank Williams, which was just getting popular about then, and the boyish sadness of football games under the lights on chill November evenings.

So I was happy, the beginning of my freshman year at Oregon State, when I got signed up for Intro to Literature. But the first thing we encountered was Eudora Welty's "The Death of a Traveling Salesman." Another defeat. Grown-up reading was incomprehensible. At first it seems hard to figure why I was so baffled by a story that these days seems direct and powerful. "Bowman could not speak. He was shocked with knowing what was really in this house. A marriage, a fruitful marriage. That simple thing. Anyone could have had that." But maybe my bafflement isn't quite so unaccountable. It is possible, given the shape of my family, there in the seventeen-year-old beginnings of my freshman year, that I did not really understand anything about the idea of a fruitful marriage. It is possible I could not yet know what the story was about.

So it is easy to imagine my surprise, a couple of years later, when my wife's father pressed me to read Hemingway, and I relented and found myself with a writer who spoke to me of what I understood to be actualities and recognizable urgencies, like the chance of dying in a pointless war (for me, the chilling possibility of going to Korea). Here was a writer who moved me to want to be like him, and to say things of fundamental consequence. If you could do that you'd never have to think you had wasted your life.

I tried to write stories in which, no surprise, everybody was doomed. I took a creative writing class from Bernard Malamud, and found that Eastern intellectuals were a breed of human being I had never imagined. Malamud met with us in a little room in a Quonset hut, and he was happy, I think. He had just published *The Natural*, and officials at Oregon State considered the creative writing class a kind of reward. Malamud had been teaching nothing but Freshman Composition.

Right off he encouraged me to write in ways that reeked even slightly of the actual world. What I did was frown my serious frown, and write up some rancher anecdotes I could claim as precious and indeed just like life. Malamud tried to tell me that my little narratives would not be stories until some one thing changed, until the consequences of a moral stance were played out. He told me there had to be a formal moment of recognition, in which the world was seen in a new way. That was how stories worked, he said, and what stories were about, learning to see freshly.

But I understood that I already saw true things about the place where I had always lived. Another true thing I thought I saw was Malamud, in his outlander's way, trying to pervert my clear heartbroken Warner Valley understandings. I would have none of his nonsense, and wrote more of my anecdotes. Malamud gave me a series of flunks, red F after red F, until I relented.

With contempt for both of us I wrote an undergraduate college story with a rising action and a recognition—all the phony works. He gave me a red A.

What a pain in the ass I must have been, and how that poor man must have shaken his head over my arrogance. But he hooked me, him and Hemingway. I was going to be a writer; that, for me, was it.

My mother hated the stiff-lipped silences commonplace in my father's family as they drove themselves toward the finally sad thing they took as success. She left eastern Oregon a long time ago, after so many years entrapped by an almost perfectly masculine economy. Women in our outback had trouble finding a person to be if they were not by nature a housemistress, a schoolteacher, or, like my aunt Vi, a leathery-handed horseback renegade who insisted on riding with the men, or maybe a voluptuary who ran to the bars in town, where at least she could find some worldly conversation and not spend her time trying to make talk with housemistresses and schoolteachers and children.

My mother tried to invent a life for herself in politics. Lately she asked me, "How did you see us?" From a mostly bedridden woman of eighty-two who almost never turns off her television, it was an important question. She seemed to mean, "Have I got it right, is that what I was?" Then she began to sputter with laughter, and told the story of going to the Eisenhower inaugural ball in 1952, Oscar in a bowler hat and black topcoat and herself in a strapless gown—a woman with huge bosoms—and how the strapless dress fell down to reveal her support garments while she sat high in a box seat looking down on the dance floor and Ike himself.

Of course I didn't remember anything about their going to

any inaugural balls. The doings of my parents were unreal as news on the radio, since I was away in Corvallis getting used to the idea of being married. And witnessing my first demonstration of academic liberalism. The man who persuaded me to take books seriously in an academic way was Herbert Childs, an English teacher at Oregon State. I came to respect his intelligence in the same blind way I allowed my father his authority, and I was almost frightened by his passion for politics. He nearly wept in the classroom when Stevenson was defeated, and to a boy from eastern Oregon it was unseemly, unmanly; I looked away. "The last good man who will ever run for president," Childs said (and maybe he was right). But I agreed with Herbert Childs right down the line. I was prime in my readiness to abandon the politics I'd inherited.

In my family we have a history of inattentiveness to one another. I had no idea my mother would pick that weekend in 1952, at Eisenhower's inaugural ball, as the emblematic moment which stood for all others: her moment "back East," the main thing to remember.

A working-class girl, my mother rose a long way, to a moment from a romance story when she sat in the same huge room with the new president of the United States, and then she was defeated and fell back into high good humor. Montaigne says virtue "is courageous, a professed and implacable enemy of sourness, displeasure, fear, and constraint, having nature for her guide, fortune and pleasure for companions." I don't want to think of my mother as merely virtuous, but she fits that description. Her saving grace is an absolute willingness to look the Devil dead in the eye, and laugh. She loves to lean back and tell you the candid truth, and turn her defeats into jokes. She said I should have seen Oscar in that bowler hat if I wanted to see something ridiculous. She wouldn't meet my eyes for a moment. I imagined she was seeing things I know nothing about. Then she turned to me, absolutely dry-eyed, and smiled.

If my mother were young again, perhaps she would own white horses and watch them run the early summer meadows down in front of our house as an evening-time storm of lightning and rain drove in from the south. Maybe she would ride one of those horses upstream along Deep Creek, toward the Warner Mountains, beyond the place where the creek leaves the highway, where she would be alone in the canyon with the vultures riding overhead on the heat waves. It would all be more than enough. Maybe she wishes she had grasped at some other life. At times I think so, and my heart is broken for her, for all of us. Yet that's my story, and not hers. She hated horses.

And then, at the age of twenty-one in January 1954, I found myself graduated with a degree in general agriculture. It is hard to imagine a more useless preparation unless you have it in mind to spend your life as a county agent deep in the Willamette Valley of Oregon.

People were dying in Korea and I was going to be drafted when I graduated. And Janet had got herself pregnant. That was how I thought of it, as something women did, not something men did to women, or women to men, but something women by themselves did for their own mysterious reasons. So I had no choice. I would enlist in the air force, where I was unlikely ever to see combat. We had put off our lives, and we could do it again. That was the thinking.

The heroism of soldiering always sounded like nonsense. It never occurred to me that dying in battle would make you more than dead. The idea of dying for a cause was stupid; if you were dead, there was nothing left, which meant you had died for nothing. That was a truth I had come to see as a child, out on the lawn in front of our house in Warner Valley, watching as the waterbirds flew north. Dying was more than anybody could ask; it was the end of such things.

Since wandering those fields as a child home from those polio hospitals, I've had one basic rule: This is my only chance, and being alive is better than not being alive. Maybe I was educated into these attitudes by the skeptical horseback men I lived with for the summers I spent on the desert. It makes me happy to think so. They knew bullshit, and they knew about the ruling class; dying for a ruling class cause was almost always bullshit. Such thinking explains my disdain for formal religion and politics. There has never been a time when I had any use for churches or assemblies. But if you carry such attitudes far enough you will be isolated from the life of your community, both helpless and unable to help.

That is part of what happened to me and, because of me, to Janet. I enlisted in the air force because I was afraid the army might send me to infantry school and what I understood (and still understand) to be pointless combat in Korea, where I might die a meaningless and premature death. Janet was pregnant. The future was with us; I had it, and I deferred it, I bargained, I persuaded Janet. Mine was a very private stance. I could remember those men in Warner Valley who endured World War II under agricultural deferments, and their ostracism. I kept my opinions to myself. I lay back. I hid out. It turned out to be a way of living at a distance from everything, with my fingers crossed behind my back. It was, as I saw it, a way of saving my life. That was the thing to keep remembering. I regarded four years in the air force as the bondage we had to endure to ensure our future. I would not be killed; instead we would kill time. Maybe I was too meek, too willing to wait, and maybe we both were. It was another failure of the imagination, and part of our ruination. We never understood that you have to save your life by making up a new one. We never got close to trusting our imaginations, nor to living by our wits.

We were young. We could have protested the pointlessness of the war as so many did a generation later, but that was not an idea I remember ever crossing my mind. It was literally unthinkable. Or we could have run away with the circus or gone to live in a whale hunter's village in the Queen Charlotte Islands. But we were passive as domesticated animals. It takes imagination and passion—driven by desire, or fear, or money—to isolate yourself and live in exile. We didn't have any of those things, and anyway it was soon too late. Not knowing what to do, we put the flesh of what we were deep in the fire, we made some innocent moves on the way to eventual divorce. But that was more than a decade later. In any event, there was nobody to blame but ourselves.

It was decided: I would be out of basic training by March, just in time to come home for the birth of our baby. But it didn't work that way.

During those years I seldom saw Pat or Roberta. When I went off to Oregon State they were children in my eyes, and to be neither seen nor heard. Then they were grown and I had no idea who they were. Not that I much cared. And anyway, there was time.

Without quite even understanding why, I was something of an outcast in high school, but Pat was a bright boy from the uphill side of town, a member of DeMolay and an honor roll student. Encouraged by my father, who wanted somebody to live the life he felt he'd been cheated out of by his father, Pat got into Stanford in the fall of 1953, with the idea of becoming an engineer. In true country boy fashion, following my father's orders, he signed up for an impossible schedule of calculus, German, the works. "Those classes were nothing but valedictorians," he said. "A couple of parties and I was two weeks behind." So he showed some style and tossed in the towel. He told of wandering out of his dorm in the early morning to see Rafer Johnson, the famous Olympic decathlon man from Tulare, heading out for a run under the eucalyptus trees on the parklike Stanford campus. Some do it, some don't. Pat's GPA at Stanford was a flat 0.00. "Got to do something famous," he would explain years later. Pat told of tearing down and putting back together a Model T in someone's dorm room, among other such schemes that sounded brilliant to me.

But my father, according to my mother, was furious about this second death of his dream. "He never forgave Pat," she told me. But I don't think that's right. By the time my father died she'd only seen him once in more than thirty years. In his last years I think he had forgiven everybody but his own father.

Roberta had gone to a private girl's school in Palo Alto, and after a couple of years in Klamath Falls, my parents sent her off to another one, in Scottsdale. She came home gloriously reprimanded, with a note saying she was "rude, crude, and socially unacceptable." But she saw it through, graduated, and lasted six weeks at the University of New Mexico before she came home to take a job in a women's store on Main Street in Klamath Falls. She was a girl, so there was nothing to forgive in my father's scheme of things.

After a couple of years running with a crowd of cronies at the University of Oregon, Pat enlisted in the army in January 1955, went through basic training at Ford Ord, and flew out to three years of working as a microwave technician in Japan. In photographs my mother took I see a tentative young man with round eyeglasses and jug-handle ears, wearing a woolen private's uniform and standing in the snow in front of the house up on Pacific Terrace in Klamath Falls. The lives of my brother and sister seemed like nothing more serious than stories to tell. Later on they told them with great glee. But both had suffered, I think, serious defeats. I was too worried about myself to even imagine their wounds. They were strangers.

In December 1953 I finished up at Oregon State. On January 14 I took a train south from Portland to Los Angeles and across the wintry deserts to El Paso and across the endlessness of Texas to Lackland Air Force Base on the edge of San Antonio. I was slated to learn some things about manhood and responsibility. At midnight the train stopped in Klamath Falls, where I was reunited with my pregnant wife for a few precious moments, and I was drunk, staggering, an inexplicable disgrace. It was a moment in which the future was foreseeable: I had money in my pocket, I was loose in the world for the first time since coming of age, and I could see no reason not to socialize in the club car with my newfound GI companions.

As our railroad train rocked along we staggered back and forth to our bunks, and then I found myself alone in the club car, confronting a gray, hung over, wised-up Sunday sunrise as we crossed the deserts of Arizona and New Mexico, talking to a black man—a conductor I suppose—who was kind to a boy like me as we gazed out to the distances and took the long view. Everyone else was sleeping in. I was beginning to be afraid.

Lackland was another dream, designed to be a dream, broken from anything you had ever counted as real. It was built on the fears of young men. The shouting started as we straggled down off the train to confront a gang of slick-faced noncommissioned officers. They studied our papers, and eyed us as if they'd unaccountably got a shipment of mooing livestock off the Southern Pacific; they shook their shaven heads and called us assholes and lined us up with some other assholes and took our packages of cigarettes and stepped on them and ground them into the asphalt.

A muscular little staff sergeant from Virginia stood us at attention and let us stand awhile and then gave us a sweetly articulated Southern lecture, walking through our ranks until he was face-on with the biggest man among us, a gangling pimpled fellow named Buzz, who had arrived with a reputation as a bad actor on Twenty-fifth Street in Ogden, Utah, a place famous at that time for railroad-man whorehouses and Mormon prizefighters. "You," the little sergeant said, "are the dumbest-looking shithead I ever saw."

Buzz swallowed, and his greaseball hands twitched.

"What do you think about that?" the little sergeant asked. "I could kick the crap out of you and send you to the stockade for a month, and then they'd ship you back here and I could do it all over again."

Buzz came from a history of repression; he didn't flinch or blink.

"That's what you and me could do. You and me, sweetheart. Right now, if you'd like to try it, Mister Shit-for-Brains, Mister Asshole."

Buzz stared straight ahead and didn't answer. We were home. We never saw this little jerk again; the opening lecture was his specialty. That night they kept us up until four o'clock learning how to make our beds with hospital corners, the stretch of GI blankets so tight you could bounce a quarter. At five-thirty we stood in cold rain and waited for breakfast; at six-fifteen, back in formation as a thin line of daybreak ran along the horizon, the rain blowing by me, I puked. Nobody paid any attention. People had troubles of their own, and we were just getting started on our first day. We were all afraid, which is how it was supposed to be.

What they do when you are a child like that is take your cigarettes and your hair and your clothes, leaving you stranded and frightened for a while before they relent just in time, right before you collapse. They give you a new tribe to live in, and you love it; they make you need that tribe and their discipline. They strip you until you become nonexistent, without enough personality to withstand even such crude brainwashing. Our man Buzz had seen some of that stuff on the streets of Ogden, but the rest of us were afraid.

It is a bad thing in our democracy that we teach our young people to find their politics in the strengths of others. We teach them to love such dependency. I loved being part of it. Because I was twenty-one, and older than anyone else, and had graduated from college, for God's sake, I was selected for leadership. They called me the squadron commander, which meant I was in charge of our little outfit when no one with any authority was around, which was most of the time. Our official drill instructor was a likable young airman third class who every day or so would come driving along in his Chrysler convertible with his handsome blond wife, just to see if we were doing all right. He had gone to Rollins College in Florida on a golf scholarship, and was quite candid about the fact that most of what he was supposed to do at Lackland was play golf with senior officers. Which he did every decent day.

So I was left in charge, to drill those poor troops, to send out road guards, to get them to chow and mail call, to settle their fights, and to make sure they polished their boots and got those beds stretched tight to their hospital corners. Buzz was my second-in-command, my enforcer. We made it through eleven weeks, which at the time seemed as important as all the history written up in Commager. I knew the face of each of my boys like a set of ugly frescoes from my dreams, and how he slept and how he marched when he was tired, and when he was too cold or too sweaty to pay attention. I knew to make sure they paid attention; I found out how to cheat the system, how to hide. It was a world, and, I see now, an education in the manipulation of authority. I was learning to be a straw boss in Warner Valley.

It didn't last. Early in March, our hair grown out a little, dressed in our airmen's basic blue uniforms, we were hauled into San Antonio and turned out to roam the dangerous streets, where temptation lived. It was my obligation to call home, but I got drunk and put it off for a day. When I did call, hung over and stupid with shame, my daughter had been born. I was in the basement of an old hotel, down by the men's room, using a pay phone. The place smelled of piss and defeat.

It had been a difficult delivery, hours and hours of pain and labor, and I'd been far away, drinking in bars with good-looking Chicano women I could barely remember.

Karen, my wife said, sounding worn out and drugged. Karen. A baby girl. We start trying to defeat guilt; we deny it. Hours in labor, my wife's courage and faith: a baby girl. What did it mean? I lied, said I'd been sick. It was true that I was sick. What did anything mean?

What should I do, now that I was so far away, in the basement of an old hotel in San Antonio, and a father?

Karen Kittredge. Her name, my family name, an ancient story I didn't understand. And I mean that. I did not know what to feel. What should I feel, what *would* I feel, if I was the right person? Maybe I could make it up. But I was not the right person, that much was clear.

I went upstairs to the bar and told my friends. We drank to my prowess and to my foolishness. It was an uneasy, two-hearted moment, one I wanted to escape: fuck you, I was thinking, fuck everybody, I'm gone from here; I'll learn, just watch; from this moment on I'm a new deal, I will be the right guy.

In the last week of basic training, I came down with dust-pneumonia and checked myself into the base hospital with a temperature of over 104 degrees. When I came out, my precious squadron had dispersed. Except for Buzz, I never saw another man of them again. It was over. I spent three days in transient barracks with the crazies and not-so-crazies who were waiting for Section Eight discharges. Some of those men would get up every morning and take a hard-on piss into their bedding, then haul the bedding over to Supply and complain, grinning all the while, "Did it again. Guess I'm hopeless."

Soon we would all be out on the streets, the game of basic training finished. I mourned; everything thereafter looked like thin going indeed. I was a married man, a father, but I was alone and deeply fearful. Always, in those days, as the air force made ready to ship me to Denver, afraid of everything.

Maybe certain possibilities looked too easily seductive: like there was an automobile, the door was open, you could slip inside and drive away forever, just vanish. Maybe it was the vanishing I feared, in the way I feared dying in Korea. Kerouac and Cassidy were boho-ing along the streets of Denver at that time and I wonder how I would've reacted if they'd ever held the car door open for me. But they didn't, and these days I don't see so much on-the-road bravado. Maybe it's just my age. Kerouac and Cassidy have been dead a long time. They would have scared me shitless.

Despite my newfound resolve, there was enough slack for some more drinking and street life before Janet came out to Denver. My GI buddies and I would go down to the black music bars at Seventeenth Street and Larimer and act knowing. Nobody bothered us, or maybe I should say bothered *with* us. It's an old story that GIs have no money.

On Easter weekend I hooked up with my old friend Buzz, and we established a quick traveling relationship with two married girls who had a car, an old convertible that belonged to the husband one of them was almost, but not quite, betraying. (Or so I thought; it depends, of course, on what you think of as betrayal.) We saw sunrise from a natural amphitheater in the Red Rocks hills, and spent Sunday afternoon in the Garden of the Gods outside of Colorado Springs. But nobody got laid, and I never saw Buzz after that. Maybe I cut him out of my life. That was enough of that; once again, I told myself, I was out on the other side of faithlessness.

It was time to reunite with Janet and confront the actuality of my daughter. A new life lay before me like a dream. How could I be a father? The air force finally gave me a few days leave time, and I flew from Denver to Moses Lake, Washington, in a cold and rattling, empty air force transport plane, hitchhiked to Euphrata, sat up all night in the lobby of a tiny hotel, caught a jammed Greyhound bus, stood in the aisle for another hundred miles, bought some civilian clothes on a layover in Ellensburg, then rode on until midnight, when I came down off another bus to the empty streets in Klamath Falls. I had been awake for most of two days. Exhausted and sorry for myself, I wanted Janet to know how I had suffered; she wanted to talk of nothing but Karen. We slowly made peace and once again learned to listen to each other, at least a little. When the baby howled for attention in the middle of the night,

I would watch in that dim light as Janet comforted her. The baby was perfect, and more than perfect. The baby was holy. Something was holy, I saw at once, and everything changed. There was something to die for.

In the early summer of 1954, when my daughter was an infant and my wife and I were both of us twenty-one, we lived on the second floor of an old house just across Seventeenth Street from City Park in Denver. In the heat of afternoon we would move out onto a screened-in porch—high up, as if we were in a secret tree house with leaves all around us, and nesting birds. Soon huge electric storms would form over the Rockies, the light turning yellow-green as those storms came sweeping down to us with drumming rain and shattering bursts of hailstones.

My daughter was a miracle. So long as you have this, I thought, you have enough, you have everything. My wife and I loved each other, it was clear.

This is a time I like to resolve into memories of tranquillity, even though I know the actual days were mostly formed around bewilderment—who were we, who should we want to be? It was the first time either Janet or I had ever lived in a city, or on our own, and we were half a continent from home.

As an airman third class, I was going to school at Lowry Air Force Base from six o'clock in the evening to midnight, training to be what was called a photo interpreter, learning to "read" aerial photographs and assess signs of damage from conventional (non-nuclear) high-altitude bombardment. A couple of years later, in the Strategic Air Command at Travis and on Guam, I got closer to what I thought of as the real stuff, high-tech radar bombsight scoring, and huge glossies of the aftermath from nuclear explosions over doomed Pacific atolls.

It was as if we were still in school and only had to make it to the next check from home, our lives an enormous distance from anything that could be considered actual. I cannot speak for the woman who was my wife; she lives far away in her own privacies. But in these latter days I find sad pleasure in recalling the summery stillness of Denver, and recall watching her push the stroller through the traffic on Seventeenth Street so she and my daughter could see the ducks ringing the edge of the pond in the park before the storms. I don't recall going with them even once.

We all lose much of what could have been ours because we don't pay much attention while we invent the future. But I have to resist telling myself that I can see that young woman and her little girl so much better in my imagination these thirty-some years after the fact than I could when they were real and I was deep in the young man's disease of looking beyond the moment. Such a notion is mostly hindsight nonsense, insulting to the people we were. A friend of mine said that the first summer he was in love exists in his memory like a church he can go visit, and those years are like that for me. We were in love, or at least trusted each other in a blind-eyed way I will never share with another adult. We were going to be together forever unto death and beyond.

My plan was to spend my air force years pursuing my secret life, reading the important books of the world and getting ready to become a writer. But when I actually seated myself before the typewriter my wife had brought to our marriage, a ranch boy with a degree in general agriculture from Oregon State College, the writing was as unreal as the air force. So I gave it up. There was plenty of time. After my time in the service I could go home to Warner Valley. First I would read all the books; then I'd know what to say.

But I didn't read anything that summer in Denver. I found solace for my anxieties in going back to boyhood, and mostly focused on building intricate model airplanes from balsa wood, breathing the fumes of strange glues while I waited for the big mysteries to dissolve and new insights to form. But those recognitions never showed themselves, and my model airplanes were ungainly and erratic in flight. Like a sulking child I would set another failure afire and sail it off our second-story porch, to crash and burn.

By August my training was finished. Given travel time and two weeks leave, I was assigned to Travis Air Force Base, on the flats south of the freeway between Sacramento and San Francisco. We loaded our old black Buick Roadmaster (next to a Cadillac the most impractical automobile we could have owned) and headed out. Our plan was to travel straight through to southeastern Oregon where, in Warner Valley, I could earn some money driving a truck for a week or so in the grain harvest and we could start taking charge of our lives again.

The drive took twenty-six hours and we brought it off in one shot, noon to two o'clock the next afternoon. I was hallucinating as I negotiated the last miles down Deep Creek Canyon and into Warner Valley, but I, at least, was home.

We stayed with my cousin Jack and Janet's sister. He and Maryann were living in his father's old house along the south edge of the valley, rooms I remembered from the old days when my father and mother and Nick and Nellie had laughed through the long Sunday afternoons and argued about the Charlie Russell prints. We were the second generation in that house, and I think we still loved and trusted one another. When we left Jack loaned me five hundred dollars—pay it back when you can, no

questions asked—and that money got us located in California.
It was easier to borrow from him than from my father.

Soon I was down in the fields, eating chaff and peat dust,
working for a man named Slim Poore. This was work I knew,
loading rebuilt two and a half–ton farm trucks from a John Deere
36 combine as it was pulled along at three miles an hour or so
by a man on an RD-6 Caterpillar. Ripe grain was shattering from
the seed heads onto the ground every time the wind blew, so
there was urgency to this task. We loaded the trucks on the
go; the combine never stopped.

When barley showed over the top of the clean grain hopper,
which meant it was full, the combine man would signal me and
I'd drop the truck into compound gear and slowly pull under
the off-loading spout. The combine man would kick in the au-
ger, and another ton or so of bright barley would spill out into
the box on the back of the truck, three or four times until the
truck was loaded and ready for someone else to drive it over
the Warner Mountains to the railroad elevator in Lakeview.

It was work I always hated because of the peat dust, which
would eat at your skin, and the long boredom of the days. But
I was making money. And I was studying Slim Poore, a gangling
taciturn man and the finest sure-thing grain farmer any of us
ever knew, a man I didn't like so much as envy.

I suppose I knew that I would never be a writer. I was already acquainted with the ominous idea that someday I would
be out of options and likely coming home to be a farmer. So I
must have been checking on Slim Poore, trying to see how his
life was livable. Maybe I thought it would do me good to take
a leaf from the book of somebody who went to the world with
such style, gray denim work clothes off the shelf from the J.C.
Penney store, shirtsleeves buttoned tight over those long wrists,
and a kind of ironic side-angle squint from under the vanity of

a white golf cap like the ones Ben Hogan wore, a new one every season.

Nothing was ever just good enough with Slim Poore, not if you could work a while longer and bring your enterprise closer to perfect; he was a man of high reputation, earned by single-minded attention and willingness. Men despised him for that diligence, but they never had his crops. For years people said it was luck, but never again after that summer in 1954. From then on you wouldn't have called him lucky.

In 1936, after the turkey-herding days in the Tule Lake country, when my family moved to the properties in Warner Valley, my father encouraged Slim to come along. After the end of World War II, when the ranch in Warner was well on the way to being paid out, my father leased Slim eight hundred acres of farming ground and ran him enough credit to set up with secondhand equipment. My father is famous for loyalties. There is an imaginable version of this story in which he was making good on what he must've considered a clear debt of gratitude for services above and beyond the call, over years. But I don't think so; I think it was mostly economics. Anytime you could get a man like Slim Poore working your ground on shares you'd be a fool not to.

And times were good, everybody prospered. And then that summer of 1954, when after sunset on my last day loading trucks in the grain field, gray peat dust hanging in the cooling air, the main brake cylinder failed on a red truck of indeterminate age. It was the sort of farm truck where the registration asks for make, and some courthouse clerk has typed in "Home-Built."

The first accident was a little thing. As I pulled the loaded truck in behind the fuel wagon, I hit the brakes—and nothing. I ran over an empty twenty-gallon grease drum in one of those slow-motion moments. I stomped on the steel brake pedal again, in the kind of careless, daydreaming way a young man will, and my old red truck kept rolling toward the tail end of the grease wagon, dumb and inexorable. It was like driving on ice in winter, and coming up on a stop sign too fast; suddenly your brakes are locked and you're coasting gently into the rear end of the car ahead. In that long moment before the little collision, your organs pump adrenaline, bringing you vividly to awareness, and you have a long slow time to *see* with such relaxed precision. All at once you are perfectly behind your eyes and a true artist of seeing.

The tail end of the grease wagon with its litter of rags and jumble of barrels was coming at me. I stomped the brake pedal another couple of times, hit the clutch, jerked the wheel, and the heavy old truck lumbered on, cutting ruts in the dry peat soil, and then I had missed the fuel wagon and an empty blue and white twenty-gallon grease drum was crunching under the wheels. One of those moments.

Slim grinned, asking me what had happened, and I told him the brakes were gone. He nodded, and we left the truck there in the falling light. It wasn't my problem. I was deep in my dread of reporting to the real air force down at Travis in a couple of days, waiting for a paycheck, already off the job.

If this were literature, precise and classical, we would know how it goes. One fatal flaw, one mistake, the combination of character, ambition, and that thing called overweening arrogance: tragedy, a good man brought down by his fate. Though the way I see it, sometimes you just risk it.

The next morning, while my wife and I were loading our Buick for the drive south into California, Slim Poore headed over the Warner Mountains to the railroad elevator in Lakeview. He was driving that old red truck, heavy with maybe four tons of barley. He hadn't fixed the brakes. His idea was to stop at the top of the pass over the mountains, stick the old truck in compound, and ease down the steep curving grades on engine compression, unload at the elevator, and get the brakes fixed in town, where they had the tools.

All that was left of the wreck, down by the little rope-tow ski area, when we got there a couple of hours before noon, was a scattering of yellow barley spilled out on the roadside grasses. My red truck with no brakes had been jerked back on its wheels and towed away. I sifted my fingers through the loose grain and guessed some of what had happened; that old truck jumping out of gear, careening down the canyon road.

Right there I might have been reconfirmed in my decision to waste four years of my life in the air force. No wrecks for me, I thought calmly. Self-possessed and aware, except that I had piled my buttery orange 45-rpm jazz records on the back window ledge of that black Buick, where they'd melted and warped in the August heat, and I don't remember caring much. Maybe I was too frightened to care about much of anything, even though we drove on without knowing that Slim Poore was unconscious in the Lakeview hospital, his back broken, crippled forever. We were heading into a new life, where they were expecting us to be adults.

Leaving Denver I'd had some choices. I chose Travis Air Force Base because it was close to San Francisco, or so you might have thought, looking at a California map. I had a vague idea about the fun we could have there. But for a GI with a couple of kids, San Francisco was as distant as the Sea of Tranquillity.

During our slow-motion years in California, when my daughter was small and I was an *airman* in all kinds of ways, we lived in the little town of Susuin, on the northern edge of the

Sacramento River delta. I settled in, and I tried to be a writer. I tried hard, a couple hundred words every night after I came home from the squadron. First I wrote a short story and sent it off to the *Partisan Review*, one of the two or three literary magazines I had ever heard of. (I don't know that I'd ever seen a copy, and I'm sure I had never actually read one.) They sent it right back, and in disdain I gave up short story writing, obviously a loser's game. I started a novel; a young man's novel about an old man, a cattle ranching hermit in Nevada who persevered, abandoned by women. Such stuff is easy to make fun of. But behind it, for me, there is another story, about an unlettered boy trying to name himself out of mythologies he detects in a backcountry culture he loves. All these stories have to do with men without women. Women, I guess, lived somewhere else, in stories about houses and families in which men were distant.

The saddest thing, however, is that I was never smart enough to see that I was living a completely different kind of life. We lived in one of those GI ghettos, long anonymous tracts of prefab houses which, after World War II, had been floated up the bay on barges from Hamilton Air Force Base, where they'd been sold as surplus. Our lives in that enclave were fractured from distant hometowns, and family was all the glue we had. Out there in that plywood housing development on the edges of Susuin Bay, our women were the philosopher-kings, and they talked security. Who could blame them, married to such hapless boys and so often pregnant with their children? Somebody should write about it; I wish I'd possessed the wit to, back when it was my life. But real life, I thought, was somewhere else. Like Hemingway's Europe, or home in Warner Valley.

Just downstream lay the wonderland possibilities of San Francisco. Which should have been a playground; I knew the way, and I understood that San Francisco was the white, logical city on the hill, the last best hope of decency where they had begun the United Nations.

The day Franklin Roosevelt died, my mother had driven the highways around Palo Alto and wept; maybe that was the day she became a Republican. A few years before, about the time I was ten, she took me to San Francisco and had me tested for intelligence. It was one of our mythologies, hers and mine, that I had tested out fine and could be expected to do well in the world just on the basis of "native abilities." My mother sat me down and told me I had an IQ that was well above normal. I believed her. A useful story, this colored my life, giving me both expectations and the belief they were not foolish. *I have a high IQ, I can have what I want if I am willing to work.*

So part of the time, at least, I tried, and was always busy dreaming up future trajectories and glories to come, dream after dream. "You can be anything," my mother said. It was her gift. She gave me a confidence which could not be entirely eroded by any of my country-headedness.

From this vantage I should have been eager to make my way over the bridges into San Francisco for at least a fling at excellence and extravagance, which might have led to maybe one night in Gino and Carlo's and a 1955 Mary-ju-anna cigarette. In another life I would learn to love the bars on North Beach. Right then they were just a boat to be missed.

San Francisco was not for children like us. We did not run up bad debts; nobody would let us. That we had no money was my first and main excuse, and my certainty that it was impossible to get any money was another failure of the imagination and will. My father never told me what to do about money. He could always create money, and more money out of that. He didn't take jobs. It's likely he didn't tell me much of

anything about the intricacies of ownership and life as it was
actually lived because he didn't think there was much to tell.
Maybe he thought money was a natural art and couldn't be
learned. Maybe he thought you would hate yourself if you were
coached.

One of my old fraternity brothers, Doug Hoagland, was
playing guard for the San Francisco Forty-Niners. I watched him
every Sunday on my new television, leading the way for what
I think of as the finest trio of running backs in the history of
the game, although they didn't win much: Joe "The Jet" Perry
and John Henry Johnson and the ultimate beauty of Hugh
McElhenny. A friend of mine, an old roommate, Doug Hoagland, was blocking for Y. A. Tittle. Think of it. An old friend.
Out there, on television. But I didn't try to call, or write a little
postcard, and then maybe drive down to San Francisco to see a
game and say hello. No. We were poor, and Doug Hoagland
was famous. His was a life properly realized; he had not abandoned himself. Thinking about Doug was a way of reproaching
myself.

What I did in the meantime, more than anything, perhaps
because it was easy, was yearn for the ownership and full possession of hardback books. I wanted to believe they were actual
in ways football was not. I still have reading lists from those
days: *Bernard Berenson, C. Day Lewis.* Each payday I traveled down
to the bookstores in Berkeley with ten more dollars set aside,
driving the fifty or so miles to Berkeley with my baby daughter
beside me in the seat of our old black Buick. I would fondle my
way along miles of shelving, touching the spines of serious books
as if I were touching women, my excitement nearly sexual, I
think. I debated weeks before purchasing the enduring pleasures
of a hardback copy of Erich Auerbach's *Mimesis.* It was so clearly
an important book, and I wanted it so much. It would tell me

so much of what I needed to know, and it did. It told me the world was made of stories, which in turn were an ultimate principle of order. But it was a long time before I understood what that meant in more than an intellectual way. I was a long time coming to see that stories were the little motors that ran our actual lives, making babies and, off in the war zones, killing them. I was too centered in ideas themselves to notice the ways they influenced conduct.

In San Francisco and around Berkeley, at that time, there were writers like Kenneth Rexroth and Robert Duncan. They were saying such important things, such as listen, learn to trust the voices who talk the language out in the townships. A boy like me, who wanted to be a writer, could have learned some things. Ginsberg and Snyder and Kerouac and that crowd were nearby. I could have been at the Six Gallery on Fillmore Street in 1955 when Ginsberg read *Howl* for the first time and his old buddy Kerouac sat on the floor slugging shots of burgundy from a bottle and singing along. "I saw the best minds of my generation destroyed by madness, starving hysterical naked."

Not me. I stayed clear. I was at Travis, playing volleyball. What did we think in those days? I recall dreaming of some life with lawns, with patios.

But I'm making us sound less substantial than we were. Those were fine, sweet times when an evening trip for ice cream all around was a major treat—and my disdain for the children we were is an act of arrogance. That girl and boy are distant people I struggle to recreate. I pity the boy I was for having been less than I imagine I could have been, and such pitying is as monstrously unfair to the people we were as it is smugly complacent for me to feel now.

My wife pushed my daughter along the quiet streets of Susuin. She was pregnant again and walked with other transient wives. My daughter was learning about the ways one residential block is much like any other. And I equivocate still.

There were questions nobody asked: unthinkable questions that would stir up fearful psychic windstorms. Nobody would've known what to say if a young man wondered aloud about the relationship between his ownership of property and his sexual possession of his young wife. Or suppose a young woman was asked to define her responsibilities to the man she had married: Should she feel obliged to see that his shirts were ironed? How should she regard his yearning for sexual adventure, in her bed and out on the living room couch and elsewhere all over town, really, if he was normal? How should she demand he react to her yearnings for the same kind of adventure, should she happen to feel such yearnings? Who belongs to whom, who owns the farm, who pulls the strings? Or the cart?

If these questions seem stupid and obvious it is because we know our answers, we have our politics rehearsed, some of us, or so we think. But when we were coming of age, Janet and I, such questions were real, and nobody even seemed to know they were questions.

Our secrets weren't really secrets, but more like blind spots. Maybe I had learned to leave such considerations to my mother and my wife. Maybe they thought such things through for all of us. It was about this time that my mother seems to have gotten ideas of moving into politics, and persuaded my father to buy a new house, up on Pacific Terrace in Klamath Falls, with the doctors and lawyers and mill owners.

But that sounds only like more pseudo-mythology about the trickiness of women. Likely nobody understood much. I knew very little beyond the most simple-minded story—*get married, have some kids, go home to the great fields in Warner, and work*—of the sort you're told when somebody like my grandfather wants you to stay quiet and useful. Such stories will encourage you to ignore what you might have been.

We owned a ticket home to Warner Valley, where we would be safe. I knew that much. The world could not hurt us in Warner Valley. That ticket home was the one thing I claimed as absolutely mine. The world owed me that much.

Like any young man I yearned for connection to huge significances. But I had no sense of destination beyond going home. I was without force. I didn't know how to conduct myself. So I did the sensible thing. I bought a black and white Motorola TV set from a cheap furniture store in Vallejo on time: one hundred and fifty dollars, with monthly payments of eleven dollars. I recall these sums exactly, because they were the first such debts I ever owed.

One spring day in March 1956, my son Bradley was born. Janet woke at three o'clock in the morning once her water had broken. She was calm and stately as she dressed, and she drank some coffee; she was experienced, a woman who knew about these things.

We got Karen out of bed (she was almost exactly two years old—two years and two days—and I've always wondered whether it was biorhythms or Janet's intentions that accounted for such regularity) and got to the hospital just in time, right before sunrise. After the nurses hurried Janet away Karen and I waited, looking at old magazines in the waiting room, but not for long. In fifteen minutes we heard a baby squalling. Karen and I looked at each other. We didn't say anything. The nurses came after me. They were smiling. A boy.

A girl and a boy. Perfect symmetry. This was a life you could trust. Janet held the baby, and we talked about names. We couldn't imagine any traditions to honor. Bradley, we finally decided. It was almost Michael, so it became Bradley Michael. Those children, Janet and I, and such chanciness. She raised them, and made it up to them, I think. I bless her.

A month later the air force shipped me out to the vast Pacific, a place called Marbo Station deep in the jungles on the north end of Guam, and closer to the possibilities of war. The men who flew the B-29s which dropped atomic bombs on Nagasaki and Hiroshima had been stationed in our buildings. I was assigned to study maplike photographs of the hydrogen bomb explosions set off on Eniwetok. Damage assessment.

I went on ahead. Janet and the children were to follow in a month or so. It was a ten-day boat ride over unimaginable expanses of ocean, to a place which was as strange as an actual nightmare. On my first trip to town I took a long path through the shadowy palm-frond jungle to the highway, sweating through my starched shirt before I made a hundred yards. On the decaying trunk of a fallen coconut tree, in stippled light only inches from my hand, something moved—the flicking tongue of a three-foot iguana. I ran, even though I knew such lizards were harmless. I had sweated through my boots by the time I made the highway.

I was supposed to be finding a house. What I did was drink beer in a tavern, then some more beer the next day, nothing really faithless, just pointless. I was a young man on his own, acting out another fantasy: sweaty young GI, far from family, sitting on a rotting plywood veranda under the coconut palms, eyeing the beautiful little brown women and sipping his booze while the slow surf rolls in from across the world.

The house I found was a rotting Quonset hut left from

World War II. There were lots of them. All you had to do was take an axe to the full-scale jungle which had grown up in the yard, put up window screens all around, lay new floors, and paint everything. Friends helped. We stole marine plywood flooring from abandoned hospital wards. I bought cases of beer, and the rooms in my house soon looked like they had been painted by impressionistic drunks: blue along this wall, green over there. I thought it was funny.

I flew back to San Francisco, to reunite with Janet and the children. At Fort Mason, after a nightmare of shots and paperwork, we were all loaded deep below the waterline into a tiny stateroom on a ship called *The Shanks*. Twelve days at the sea, dripping with sweat and with two boat-sick children, and then the vivid green beauty of our island. There is nothing more lovely than a Pacific island seen on the horizon. Up close it was another thing: 100 degrees, 102 percent humidity, gecko lizards on the walls, eating ants. The house was unlivable. Janet didn't think it was funny at all. She wept for a couple of days and then she took charge.

And the world took pity. A friend of a friend turned out to know a master sergeant from Base Supply who was shipping out. We got his house on the hill above a town called Taumuning. We had a lawn, neighbors, a swingset, and a trail which looped through the second-growth jungle to an overlook where red volcanic cliffs dropped fifty or so feet to red boulders and the roll of sea. The Japanese machine gun emplacements on the cliffs had concrete walls six feet thick. Inside there was a tiny place where the gunner could sit and fight off the rats and keep watch over the ocean through narrow slits, gazing out to the island of Rota, and wait. A thousand miles beyond lay Japan, the dark Orient, history. We weren't interested. We were looking for a home.

The only pane of glass in the house was the bathroom mirror. During typhoons we would be doused by sprays of wind-driven rain and salt water coming over the cliffs from the thundering house-high breakers. Our first month we took in a kitten. The second month we got a rat, a huge fellow who gnawed his way in through the baseboard in the kitchen. I beat at him with a broom, and then the kitten came off the top of a partition like an angel and I watched and applauded the idea of killing without possibility of remorse. Our house was safe.

In the morning our front porch would be covered with snails in huge yellow-gray shells. They had been imported, as food, by the Japanese; sometimes a creature called the coconut crab lived in these shells. I would step carefully between and around them, and then one would run away, pincers clattering on the deck like something out of a horror movie. Sick with fever, tossing on the bed where we never slept under more than a sheet, I looked at a window and saw a huge lizard framed there on the outside of the screen. Nightmares, but who cared. We played canasta with new friends, a couple named Broderick. It was essential to have best friends, and I found it difficult to keep pretending my writerly obsession was real and not just another way of fucking around.

Then came the killer, as they say. One bright morning I went off with a young Guamanian GI who had grown up not far from the base. We were detailed to cut a twenty-foot bamboo mast for the squadron sailing ship. This was a considerable task, but also an adventure and something of a reward, a day of escape from routine. I was the driver; my Guamanian companion, a thin boy with a lovely wife and wispy mustache, was my guide. The bamboo grew in thickets near his childhood home. We parked our GI six-by-six truck in front of that backlands shanty house—nobody seemed to be home but it turned out they were hiding—and ventured into the shadowy lizard-green light inside enormous groves of bamboo.

What next happened was simple. My companion fell into an epileptic seizure, down there in the bamboo, after we'd cut our mast, and I ran from him as if he'd turned satanic. He had, some part of me intuited, gone to an animal place I didn't want to know about. As I gathered myself and did what I was honor-bound to do—go back and, according to first aid, get a stick between his teeth—I was as afraid and unwilling to touch him as I would have been with a shrieking bat. I carried him up the hill to the house where he'd grown up, which was now streaming with people, his weeping exotic wife and his grandmother, an old woman who told me to lay him down, this had happened before. Then she told me to leave, and I did. I went back to the base and told our commanding officer we had a medical emergency.

This was a story I played like a joke, my running away, and how frightened I was. But I couldn't make myself really think about it. A week or so later I saw that Guamanian boy at some base ceremony and we didn't speak. A door had opened, and I had been shocked by a sight of what I took to be chaos just at the end of the hallway. That glimpse of what I took to be the unknowability of things cost me some decades—or maybe not. It's hard to figure. Maybe it made me alive. I have no idea what it cost the Guamanian boy.

Everything that is interesting, Céline says, happens in the shadows. We seldom attempt talking about our real concerns, or even bring them out into the light. I think he is at least partway right. There seems to be a long gap between much of what drives us and the things even the most daring of us are willing to bring up in conversation. We are not easily capable of thinking or talking about the possibility that our lives make no rational sense beyond the answering of animal needs—or that the comforts of such a life might be enough. Think of hot summer nights and waking up one morning to soft cool rain falling into the trees outside the open windows, and making love in the dim light.

I recall the strobe-light discordances of my childhood jazz clubs, and the streaks of sundown light across the floors of old taverns with their doors standing open to summer, places I still adore. What I like in my memories of those jazzy places and what I still find useful in taverns is the way they encourage me to love what I can understand. Then I think of the edges of morning as I remember them from that specific time down in the bamboo lowlands, the green light vibrating around me like shattered glass. Years later I gave in to my terror of what I saw that morning. The bamboo lowlands were swollen with moment, but it was no energy that I could name, so I found it frightening. I saw a fragility in myself that seemed incomprehensible and I still cannot focus my mind on it except to admit, as I put it from my mind one more time, that I am flinching from what should be one of my tasks were I ever very useful. At that time I was convincing myself that my notions of being a writer were the daydreams of a spoiled child. So I gave it up. To cherish the perfection of my children, I thought, was enough.

We went to movies in an outdoor theater, where we sat on benches. It always rained, but we had slickers. I saw Gregory Peck through his ridiculous turn as Ahab with rain dripping off the brow of my slicker. It seemed right.

My friend Ken Broderick had grown up in eastern cities, working as a union printer. He had a Doberman and kept the world at some distance, seeming to regard the life he had discovered when the air force sent him to South Dakota as a kind of gift, maybe the only real gift he would ever get. On weekends we went out into the jungles and stripped the radiators from abandoned World War II jeeps, most of them wrecks. We sold the radiators to scrap dealers who crushed them and sold them by the shipload to the Japanese. This seemed, back then, a supreme irony.

We spent the money on beer, or we saved it up and spent it on Christmas, which we celebrated with friends at our house, some of them alcoholic lifers from the squadron. Our Quonset hut on the hill above Taumuning, with me and Janet and the babies, had become the home you came to, an actual shelter, and we were sharing it.

Marriage, it was clear, was the safe place. Marriage cherished itself. Not long after, I began designing houses. I bought a drawing board and graph paper and a T-square and a 45-degree plastic triangle and some magazines that carried house plans; I studied them, and redesigned them, angling for a lineup of rooms which would lead you to live in perfect ways. What I was after was a story we could inhabit, ourselves and nobody else, my wife and me and our babies, in which we, and she and I, could love each other and be sure nothing was wrong. What I wanted was some dreamlike Frank Lloyd Wright bungalow where we could sit on the veranda forever and it would always be twilight in the temperate zones, in the most beautiful house.

Our time in the air force was ending, and the future could begin. That was what Janet and I mainly saw, I think, and we were happy enough in our lives, on the alert, ready to stand off foreseeable evil. In some way I was quitting on myself as I opted to go back to the ranch—I knew it—but that was all right, time was like a swing that only swung you back and forth.

In these memories I am a presence like smoke, almost invisible. Maybe it is because I gave myself so completely, for a short while, to that marriage. Maybe I gave myself away for the only time in my life, a time which could also be described as best. Or maybe that is sentimental, and too hard on what came afterward.

CHAPTER 6

WHO OWNS
THE WEST?

During our last months on Guam, my mother wrote to tell us that she and my father were determined on divorce. Their care for one another had run aground on my mother's ambitions and my father's sense of betrayal. At least that's how I chose to understand the story.

Such dislocation seemed crazy, and I didn't want to know the details. They would have nothing to do with the sureties of my life. I needn't have worried. My mother didn't tell much in her letters, and my father never said anything.

So it was only when I started piecing this book together that my mother sat up in bed, shut off the television, and told me her version of what had happened. Or at least tried. After so many years I still couldn't get myself to listen with a purely receptive ear. What I got turned out to be a story of what happened to my father. I don't know my father's version. I never had the guts to ask if he had one for the telling. I don't think I could bear the intimacy of hearing my mother tell me what happened to her.

For years my father suffered from an infection of the urinary system. Everybody thought it was cancer, and that it would kill him; but it wasn't, and it didn't. He was incapacitated and had to take leave from the ranch, and he was mostly off the property for four years, fishing at Odell Lake when he felt good, and as my mother said, "just fooling around." A hired manager took his place. "Those were the best years we had," my mother said, and she brightened and remarked that it was curious those were years without much sex. I stopped listening. "We had always been very sexual," she said. Ask for truth and what do you get? Candor.

Then my father got well, and when he heard that my grandfather had fired the hired manager, he decided to go back to the ranch. According to my mother, he just loaded his stuff in the car and headed for Warner, without talking to anyone, to take over the farming again, like he hadn't missed a beat. I find it hard to imagine he could have been that simple-minded. In any event, it didn't work out.

The central argument in my family sprang from disagreement about the economic relationship between the cow-and-calf business and my father's new-age kingdom, which was called the grain camp, or the farming, another version of the old quarrel between herders and plowboys, cowboys and nesters, driven by the historic disdain of free-roaming hunter-gatherers for those who settled to muck for crops in the mud. In my family it was mostly centered on ego and style, power and—always, ultimately—money.

It's easy enough to predict the consequences, in hindsight. But you have to be careful with these stories. Here's one version. After the big World War II grain prices had mostly paid off the mortgages on the ranch at Warner, after years of high living, my father got into his health problems and a manager was hired to take his place. When my father was cured, and the manager was fired, he decided it was time to go back to Warner. My grandfather met him on the highway, flagged him down, and told him to go home. The job wasn't his anymore. He was fired, call it officially retired. I try to imagine that showdown by the roadside, father and son, grandfather and father, leaning on the fender of the older man's gray Cadillac. Maybe they just shouted at one another, all their anger coming to a wild new focus. However it happened, this break was irrevocable, the second tragedy of my father's life. The first was his decision, again on his father's say-so, to give up law school and stay with ranching.

My grandfather told my father that Jack Nicol was going to be calling the shots at Warner. Jack had been training for a couple of years. It was time the work was passed on to another generation, time for a young man. My grandparents had raised Jack after his mother died, and he became the hope of my grandfather's life after my father turned out to be a bad son and an irresponsible playboy. Jack would be the responsible son and the great cattleman; and, unlike my father, he was someone my grandfather could control.

"Afterward, he wanted his father dead," my mother said, talking about my father, "and I don't blame him. He said he'd run him down if he saw him walking beside the road. What he should have done was have some guts and go to court."

My mother and his friends encouraged him to run for the State Senate, and he lost, and said he was glad he lost, and my parents split. It's easy to imagine the melodrama. My mother was the one with political ambitions. It's my guess she drove my father much like my grandfather was trying to drive all of us. It's likely she was sick of him when he lost, and perhaps disgusted with herself. Later she ran for the House of Representatives a couple of times herself, using up many of her resources. When that failed, as such hopes in a woman were bound to fail in the political world of that time in the West, she turned passive and defensive, never quite bitter and still quick-minded but retired from ambition. She collected jade.

Our lives are dreams. Hers were not coming true, and who knows what my father was dreaming? Janet and I didn't understand much of this story at the time, and I'm not sure we would have done anything different if we had. In October 1957 I got out of the air force, and mostly because I lacked the will to take life in a more imaginative direction, we headed straight to Warner. By that time the safe thing had become a habit. It was another run to cover—this time for life, so we thought—and a mistake all the way.

It's unhappy to talk of yourself in terms of shrinking from the world, but we did, reasoning that we didn't know where else to go, with the children and all. I don't recall giving much thought to a more ambitious set of plans. We were family and they had to find a place for us, that much was sure. At least that was what I thought.

My grandfather, I'm sure, wasn't necessarily happy about having me (my father's son, after all) anywhere on the property. But Jack was new to his responsibilities (and I think he was trying to be fair, and we had a history of friendship, and Maryann was Janet's sister). He gave us the house which had been my father's guest house, and spent some money fixing it up for a family—a kitchen with Formica countertops, a new bathroom, the works. By January 1958, Janet was settling into her ranch-wife role and I was laboring as a hand in the fields in exchange for the house, food from the company storerooms, and $250 a month. Fair enough, everybody told me, since I didn't know how to do anything and, as one of the old hired men said, my hands were soft like a baby's.

My brother and sister showed up too late for the party—maybe they were born too late. Pat and Roberta were essentially invited to find other lives. There was no room for them in the hierarchy at Warner. Roberta was never a factor—she was a girl, and in our way of proceeding it was understood that girls married and followed their husband to his destination. Which she did, by marrying a wild redheaded boy from Bly named Rex Dillavou, who worked as a produce man for Safeway.

In early December 1957, I was in Oakland, picking up our household belongings off a ship from Guam, when Pat came home from Japan. I went to the Oakland army depot, the only one from our family there to welcome him, and stood by the gangplank as hundreds of uniformed young men bearing duffel bags came down into the arms of their loved ones. I didn't recognize him. Stationed for a couple of years on the outskirts of Nagoya, Pat had put on a lot of weight. A skinny kid had shipped out, and a heavy young man had come home. "Bill," he said. It took me a long moment to see my brother inside that GI stranger.

I sorrowed a little for my lost youth as I listened to his stories of saki-drinking rituals and eating exotic uncooked fish and endless GI partying. Not for me, I thought, in my most self-congratulatory and merciless good-citizen mode. Pat, it seemed to me, had gone fleshy and been partway ruined; it was clearly his own fault. I'm sure I seemed as distant to him. Again, old mythologies: brothers go out questing into the world and learn to dream different dreams. But in the master-myth of families, at least one of them is supposed to come home bearing wisdom.

Pat tells of circling the Klamath Falls airport a few days

later, after being processed through the discharge procedure. The bare hills were gray and muddy, patched with snow, the sky heavy, dark smoke swirling over the lumber mills. "I thought, this is home? After Japan it was like landing on the moon." Now he's a lawyer with an office above Main Street, just across from the county courthouse in Klamath Falls. *Raw towns,* Yeats says, *that we believe and die in.*

We were raised to believe work done well would see us through. The rewards of labor, it seemed, would be rationed out with at least a rough kind of justice. We were willing to trust in the native straightness of things. It didn't work out. We were like children in my family—all of us, I think, my grandfather and father included—unlettered and uninstructed, knowing little of our own history, never suspecting the degrees to which we were failing to understand our situation. For a little while we owned an empire, and that fact taught us to protect our interests by hardening our hearts against one another. I don't know if I would have understood, but it might've helped if someone had taken the trouble to tell me what was going on inside the councils of my family, something so simple as who had come to hate whom, and why. Knowing the score would have helped in a practical sense. But nobody did.

Going back to Warner was a grand turning point in my life, and a mistake that cost me a decade. I made it in ignorance, trusting in the goodness of my own family, which I would never do again. I can't speak for Janet, but it took me much more than a decade to swallow my bitterness. We didn't have any other options that we understood, but I think we were owed the real story of what was going on, and which deals were already salted down. Maybe we would have moved on before so much was wrecked. But likely not.

In the spring of 1958, at home in their big rock house in

Klamath Falls, my grandfather and grandmother sat down to a pinochle game with old friends. My grandfather fell out of his chair, into a stroke. A few days later he was dead, and everything was changed.

At Warner we were in the midst of the farming twenty-four hours a day. It was a time of great disturbance and excitement. I don't remember grieving for the old man at all; rather, I was frightened and exhilarated. Everything was changing, and I was going to be part of plans for the future. Jack was in Klamath Falls, seeing to the details of the dying. I was left in charge of the farming, and I loved it; working daylight to dark, talking to Jack on the telephone almost every day, and doing as I was told, detail by detail. The sweet spring days turned by, the men on the machinery fell to their work as if it was the purpose they'd always been intended for, and the result was the finest grain crop I ever planted. It was no mystery to me that I was destined to be a great farmer, and that was hugely important to a boy who had never been much good at anything.

At that same time, Jack's power in the company was being formalized and consolidated, and our relationship was soon to follow the rules of unnatural selection and survival of the fittest. We were done with boyhood and its enthusiasms. The Warner Valley Stock Company shares were divided into five equal blocks, one each for my grandfather, my grandmother, my father, my aunt Viola Gouldin, and Jack by way of his mother. Upon my grandfather's death Jack inherited his fifth, which meant Jack owned two fifths outright; he also controlled my grandmother's share, which gave him three fifths of the votes on any issue. At that point he was in charge of the family business. One of the first things he did was promote me to boss of the grain camp.

My pay doubled, I was issued a company gas card, and Janet

was given the privilege of charging anything she wanted, no questions asked, at a grocery store in town. For a swing of seasons I was awash with a young man's arrogance and pride. I was one of the men running the MC, one of the paradigm ranches in the American West; I was hot shit, hiring and firing and buying and selling and only twenty-six.

In the meantime there was my father, his work gone, divorced from my mother, and effectively disinherited. And some of his oldest friends, like Henry Nicol, were already dead. So he drank. When he heard I was running the grain camp at Warner, having taken the job without so much as consulting him, he must have felt I had gone over to the enemy. But he never said anything. I was transfixed by the glories of my new life, running the dream which had once been his. I don't recall any sense of dis-ease as I moved classically into my father's place in life. Everyone I talked to seemed to think it was proper I should take the job, and I was easily persuaded. My father was worn out; I was young and energetic. His feelings were not an issue. Most families, I think, like animals, are not so much cruel as driven by instinct. My king was dead.

For eight years I was the farming boss at the MC. Those crops and that irrigation system were the finest playthings of my life. We were making something be as perfect as it could be in our notion of the world, and for a long time I loved it. All at once we were the adults, entrusted with power. We thought we were doing hugely important work, remaking the world on an image borrowed from efficiency experts. We drained the wetlands and thought that made them ours. We made ditches and named the ditch corners—Four Corners, the Big Pump, Center Bridge, Beatty Bridge—and we thought such naming made the valley our own. The road into the valley was paved; we had electricity and television, and the animal-centered agricultural world I had grown up in was mostly gone just like that. That quickly.

The ranch was being turned into a machine for feeding livestock. We had leveled thousands of acres for alfalfa, and we kept leveling more; the swamps were drained, and the thronging flocks of hundreds of thousands of waterbirds were diminishing year by year; the hunting was still fine if you had never seen anything else, but we knew better.

Our irrigation system was a masterpiece of complexity with more than five thousand water control devices, headgates, valves, eighteen-inch pumps. We could run the water around and around in that system on a dry year, pumping it back up to re-irrigate with—until it wore out, was the joke. For a number of years the main part of my work in the spring of the year was that system, a twenty-four-hour-a-day job called "balancing water."

People keep telling me I should reread *The Cherry Orchard* and "The Bear," which they think of as the literature of giving up on property. But right then we weren't giving up on anything. We were like the Snopses; we took and ached to own more. Except it didn't work, really. We cut our alfalfa with swathers, baled it with five-wire balers. Harrow-Beds picked up the bales from the field and stacked them mechanically. We sprayed 2-4-D ethyl and malathion and the World War II German nerve gas called parathion (for clover mites in the barley), working to shorten our own lives. We baited the coyotes with 1080 and hunted them from airplanes; we wiped them out. The rodent population exploded and field mice destroyed our alfafa. We irrigated and re-irrigated, pumped and drained; our peat soil began to go saline.

We couldn't hire anybody who cared enough about our mechanical work to do it right. The old men, who had learned the rules of this life during the Great Depression, were dying, and not many young men were coming to the work with anything but disdain. Men who hired out as ranch hands in the 1960s were missing the boat, and they knew it. They despised themselves for it. And they despised the work.

Up on the hill above the old buckaroo camp we built an industrial plant called the feed mill, a space-age collection of steel buildings which housed an interlinked system of rollers and grinders and blowers and chain drives and augers and hundred-horsepower electric motors, a huge grain storage bunker, and endless lots for fattening cattle. Each year we shipped around five thousand fat animals to be butchered. The feed mill was designed to chop hay and roll grains and mix in additives from molasses to growth-inducing chemicals like stilbestrol. It was a howling, stinking place where the work proceeded at the pace of the machinery.

In winter those thousands of animals, penned into that long reach of lots, waiting for the feed truck to come down the aisle and eventual slaughter, were adjunct to the feed mill, which was the arm of our intentions gone mechanical. In spring we cleaned the manure from the lots with D-7 Cats and scrapers. It was our dream that had led us to these processes.

After a half mile in soft rain on the slick hayfield stubble, I would crouch behind the levee and listen to the gentle clatter of the waterbirds talking and then surprise them into flight, maybe a half-dozen mallard hens and three green-headed drakes lifting in silhouetted loveliness against the November twilight, hanging only a half-dozen yards from the end of my shotgun. This was called jump-shooting, or meat-hunting, and it almost always worked. But I wish someone had told me reasons you should not necessarily shoot. I wish I'd been told to kill ducks only once or twice a winter, for a fine meal with children and friends, and that nine times out of ten I was going to be happier if I let the goddamned birds fly away.

But I was at the peak of my boyish, energetic powers and just that moment happy as such a creature can be, prideful with young ambition. I was centered in the world of my upbringing; deep into the management of perfection. I was the boss at the grain camp. It was my responsibility to run the ranch-hand cookhouse and supervise the labors of ten to twenty-five workmen. Or, to phrase it most crudely, as was often done, "hire and fire and work the winos."

Think of it as a skill, learnable as any other. As in any profession there are rules, the most basic being enlightened self-interest, a code I'd begun learning at Lackland, marching my flight of newcomers to the air force. Take care of your men and they will take care of you. Understand their frailties, because you're the one who's responsible for taking care. But my duties at Warner were more profound. These men might fall sick to death in the bunkhouse. It was my responsibility to call someone who could administer mercy. What attention, I wondered, should I give them as they died?

Some thirty-six miles west of our valley, over the Warner Mountains in the small lumbering and ranching town of Lakeview, a workmen's hotel functioned as a sort of hiring hall. There was a rule of thumb about the men you would find there. The best of them wore a good pair of boots laced up tight over wool socks, which meant they were looking for a laboring job; those wearing low-cut city shoes with no socks and no laces were flat hapless, only looking for a place to hide, and never to be hired. It was a rule that worked.

My father had set up the grain camp on a sagebrush hillslope beneath a natural spring on the west side of Warner Valley. And it *was* an encampment, short on every amenity in the early days except running water—a double row of one-room shacks, eight in all, trucked in from a logging camp in the late 1930s. Two more shacks were tacked across one another in a T-shape to make a cookhouse, one for the cooking and the other for the long table where everyone ate.

The men who lived two to a cabin in the busy seasons, sweltering on that unshaded hillslope in the summers and waking in the night to the stink of drying work clothes as they fed split wood to their little stoves in the winter, were a mix of transients and what we called homesteaders, men who stayed with us for more than an occasional season, often years in cabins which eventually became known as theirs. Those men have my heart; they were my friends and my mentors. Some of them died at the grain camp and have been inconspicuously dead for many years: Louie Hanson, Vance Beebe, Jake O'Rourke, Lee Mallard, so many others.

When I came to my job as boss of the grain camp, in the spring of 1958, I was twenty-five years old, done with college and the air force and back to my beginnings after eight years away, filling my father's shoes. I was a woeful figure from American business mythology, the boss's kid soon to inherit a property he didn't know anything about, who didn't even know there was nothing to inherit.

There was no choice this side of disgrace but to plead justifiable ignorance and insinuate myself into the sympathies of the men. Ceremony demanded I show up twice a day to sit at the head of the long table for meals, breakfast and noon, and in the course of those appearances legislate my way through the intricacies of managing eight thousand acres of irrigated land. For a long time I was bluffing, playing a hand I didn't understand, risking disgrace and reaping the predictable whirlwind.

The man who saved my bacon was an alcoholic old Swede in filthy coveralls named Louie Hanson, who sat at my right hand at the table. Louie had worked for my father since our beginnings in Warner, hiring out as a catskinner in 1937, to build dikes with that secondhand Caterpillar RD-6, the first track layer my father bought, and made his way up to Cat mechanic and into special prerogatives, one of which was some drinking.

Theoretically, we didn't allow any drinking at all. Period. Again, there were rules. You need to drink, go to town. Maybe your job will be waiting when you get back, maybe not. Unless you were one of the old hands, whose jobs were secure. But nobody was secure if they got to drinking on the job, or around camp.

Except for Louie. One late May afternoon in my early childhood, one of those days when my father took me on the levee-bank roads with him as he admired his drill rows of grain newly sprung from the earth, a cold and windy day, we came across a 150-acre plot of seeded ground which was flooded under maybe a foot of water. A headgate had been opened by mistake, drowning the crop; an expensive proposition.

An old Jeep pickup was coming toward us, driven by Louie. Sometime in the last couple of days he had opened that head-gate and flooded the field before us. He was drunk. Louie stopped beside my father's pickup, rolled down the window, and faced the music with a wide shit-eating grin. "Hell, Oscar," he said, *"you* get drunk."

"Sometimes," my father said, "I sober up."

That was it. They both drove on. My grandfather wanted Louie run off the ranch, but my father would hear none of it. He was legendary for the good regard paid him by other men; nobody ever doubted that he was honest and would treat you as decently as you deserved, and maybe better. When Louie Hanson died he had given our family half of his lifetime, with little coming back beyond a room in the bunkhouse and board and subsistence wages. He was my main counselor.

A crew that hangs more or less together through seasons is like family, with a soul that is pounded by the same blows which are inevitable in any family, such as leaving and death and power.

At the grain camp in Warner Valley we ate at what could be called a family table; it was the center of a ritual, a healing ceremony of sorts, where we solved our problems and planned away our troubles. And there was never a doubt who was boss—it was me, at least until dinner, and then it was important that the men eat without me according, I suppose, to rules of their own. I thought it was important that they have that much freedom if they were to respect themselves.

Around five-thirty on a routine morning, after a hot shower and instant coffee, I would drive three or so miles to the grain camp. The best cabin, walls filled with sawdust for insulation, was where Louie lived. Every morning in winter he would go down to the Cat shop to build his fire before breakfast, then dig a couple of beers from one of the bolt-rack cubbyholes, pop the tops, and set the bottles on the stove to heat. Once they were steaming he'd drink them down in a few long draughts, all set to seize the day.

So it would not be an entirely sober man I greeted when I came early to breakfast and knocked on the door of his cabin. Louie would be resting back on the greasy tarp that covered his bed, squinting through the smoke from another Camel, sipping coffee from a filthy cup and looking up to grin. "Hell, come in," he would say. "You own the place."

Louie would blink his eyes. "You got enough water in Dod-

son Lake?" He was talking about one of the huge grain fields
we flooded every spring. And I wouldn't know exactly what he
meant. Louie would look at me directly. "South wind, and you're
going to lose some dikes." I knew what that meant: eroded levee
banks, washouts, catastrophe, 450 acres of flooded alfalfa.

Up at the breakfast table, while Louie reached for the
pounded round steak, I would detail a couple of men to start
drawing down the water in Dodson Lake, a process involving
the opening of huge valves, pulling headgate boards, running
the eighteen-inch pump. All of which would have been unnec-
essary if I'd known what I was doing in the first place. Which
everybody knew and nobody mentioned. A cheap mistake, easily covered: wages, electricity to run the pump, wasted time,
maybe a couple hundred bucks. Without Louie's intercession,
maybe twenty thousand.

The fall of our first year back on the ranch Janet and I took the
children and drove to Eugene, where my mother and brother
were living in very separate ways. My mother was set up in
some elegance in a new suburban house with antique furniture
and new dishes, the works. She seemed absolutely secure, back
in charge of herself now that she was finished with catering to
my father's needs. Pat had gone back to living what she considered scandalous and pointless sleep-till-noon bachelor-pad high
jinks while making another pass at the University of Oregon.
Older brother to the prodigal son, I was envious; Pat's irrespon-
sibilities and wastrel days and nights looked appealing to someone as tightly bound to family as I was. His friends were
endlessly funny, some of the girls they knew were pretty, and
they were free to sit up all night drinking beer and listening to
Jonathan Winters records if they wanted to.

But we gathered together and loved one another anyway, and then drove over to Florence, where Roberta was living her suburban life with her husband, Rex Dillavou. She was as contained as I ever saw her, maybe just for that while, as her children were being born, thinking she had the future locked. Rex had been promoted to manager of the local Safeway; he was handsome and energetic and down to business, the sleeves of his white shirt rolled over his freckled forearms. We went fishing, we drank some whiskey, and we had a hell of a good time. We were on our way to the store for candy, all of us.

Or maybe not. Maybe spooks were already collecting. Janet and my mother took the children back to Eugene, and Pat and I made a swing past the homecoming football celebration at Oregon State. The boys out together. I loved it. Downtown afterward, in the Benson Hotel in Corvallis, we were drunk. I babbled incoherencies but I hadn't run crazy in years, and it felt good. Later I was ashamed, wondering what my old college friends must have thought. They were wearing suits and buying houses in Portland, moving out into the world. Maybe I was wrong about the ranch. Maybe I was wasting my life.

The deeply fearful are driven to righteousness, as we know, and they are the most fearsome fools we have. I had been boss at the grain camp for four or five years, and had come to understand myself as a young man doing good work, employing the otherwise unemployable (which was kind of true). I also counted myself as a man whose efforts were continually confounded by the incompetence of the people who worked for him. I was bursting with self-importance.

We were farming twenty-four hours a day through early May while the Canada honkers hatched their downy young and the tulips pushed up through the crusted flower beds and the Lombardy poplars broke their buds and the forsythia bloomed lurid yellow against the cookhouse wall. But I don't recall such glories when I think of those spring mornings. I remember the odor of dank peat turning up behind those disc Cats as we went on farming twenty-four hours a day, and how much I loved breaking ground.

Most mornings I'd wake up before sunrise and go piss, then stand in my undershorts on the screened-in veranda attached to the house where I lived with my wife and young children, shivering with chilliness and happiness as I smelled the world coming alive. Far out across our valley the lights on our D-7 disc Cats would flicker as lights do when seen through a screen, moving almost imperceptibly. I would take my binoculars and open the screen door and gaze out at those lights as if I might catch one of my night-shift catskinners at some dog-fuckery, but really all I wanted to see was the machinery moving. Those track layers would clank along all through the hours of darkness at two or three miles an hour, turning a thirty-six-foot swath, a hundred acres every night and another hundred on the day shift. The upturned soil would mellow in the air for a day, and then we would harrow and seal it with dust, and drill it to barley. In ten days or so the seedlings would break earth, and those orderly drill rows undulating over the tilled ground toward the sundown light were softly yellow-green and some growing thing I would see to completion.

It came to a couple hundred acres of barley every day for fifteen days, about three thousand acres in all. By the end of harvest in late September, at roughly a ton per acre, that came to three thousand tons of barley at fifty dollars a ton. In our end of the world, in the early 1960s, $150,000 was real money.

The man I call the Murderer was one of those on the disc

Cats, circling toward the sunrise. Our involvement had started the previous fall when someone from the Oregon State Parole Board called and asked if we would participate in what they called their custody release program. They would send us a parolee if we could guarantee a job; in return we got an employee who was forbidden to drink or quit, on penalty of being sent back to prison. If "anything" happened we could call the state police to come take him away. This setup seemed like a fair idea; it had been twenty years since the Murderer had killed his wife in an act of drunken bewilderment he couldn't recall.

Pensive and bruised and looking incapable of much beyond remorse, he spent the winter feeding bales to the drag at our feed mill, a cold and filthy job, and as monotonous an enterprise as it is possible to imagine this side of automation. So when it came time to go farming in the spring, I sat him up at the controls of an RD-7, taught him to pull frictions and grease the rollers, and called him a catskinner, which is to say, I gave him some power. The Murderer responded by starting to talk. Frail and dark-eyed in a stiff new evergreen-colored work shirt with the sleeves rolled to expose thin white arms, he was full of bright, misinformed chatter at the breakfast table.

All I remember is annoyance. Then it rained, and we couldn't work. My crew went off to town for a couple of days with my blessing, and the Murderer went with them. That was against our rules, his and mine. When he turned up at breakfast drunk, frightened, and unable to be sober, he was lowering himself into my mercies, which did not exist. I fired him on the spot.

Only in the imagination can we share another person's specific experiences. I was the ice man, which means no stories, please, no forgiveness for you and there never will be, just roll your goddamned bed and be gone. If I fired him, he would go back to prison. I knew that. I'm sure I imagined some version of his future isolation, and his wrecked recognition that in this life he was not going to be forgiven. Stories bind us by reminding us that our lives all exhibit the same fragilities, and thus demand that we stay humane. But I didn't want to be humane; I wanted to be correct. If I hadn't ignored his devastation as I no doubt imagined it, I might have found a way to honor common sense and take him riding around with me that day as he sobered up, listening to his inane babbling. But I sent him down the road, and thought I was doing the right thing. There were rules.

My friend from Guam, Ken Broderick, had gone on to raise minks in the hills outside Rapid City. Once he brought his wife to visit us in Warner, with the idea he might take a job working for me, but he went back to his adopted hills, never to be heard from again. I thought he valued independence in ways that were unrealistic, but now I suspect he simply fled the sorry prick he saw in me. As I tell these stories I mean to say, See, I am not like that anymore. But we know that is only another tale.

I fired a lot of men, and Louie Hanson more than once, after on-the-job binges. But Louie wouldn't go away; he knew the true nature of our contract. I needed his assurances exactly as he needed his life at the grain camp. After a few days Louie would sober up and come morning he'd be sitting at the breakfast table like nothing had happened. He was fired, in fact, the day he died. He was too drunk to make sense by three in the afternoon, feeding shots of whiskey to the chore man, which meant I had to take some action, so I told him to clear out. What he did was go off to visit an old woman he'd known years before in a small town just down into California.

"A fancy woman," Louie said after drawing himself up to a fine, old-man lewdness. "Screw you, I'm going to see a woman I should've been seeing." He was seventy-seven years old and, so far as I knew, unkillable, as he drove away in his old Plymouth, squinting through his cracked eyeglasses.

A stranger in a pickup truck hauled him home late that night. Louie had wrecked his car and he was ruined himself, cut over one eye and hallucinating as he lay curled into himself like an old knot right on the floor, reeking with vomit, not even willing to open his eyes, complaining that his glasses were lost. This descent into nowhere had happened before. Let him lay. And he did, after climbing into his bed, facing the wall for three days.

By then it was clear something extraordinary and terrible was afoot, but Louie refused to hear of the hospital in Lakeview. They kill you, he said. Around the time of World War I, in the Imperial Valley of California near Calexico, his back was broken when a bridge caved in under a steel-wheeled steam tractor. The doctors got him on morphine for the pain, then fed him alcohol to get him off morphine. That was it for the rest of his life. Booze.

They just left me there, he would say, half drunk and grinning like it was a joke. Maybe he felt the doctors had already killed him. I called his son in Napa, California, who came overnight in an old car and talked Louie onto his feet, as I should have done, and into a trip over the Warner Mountains to the hospital.

All that should have been my responsibility. Days before, I should have ignored his objections. Doctors wouldn't kill him. He would have lived some more, not for long maybe, but a while. But such obligations were beyond my job description. I fell back on excuses.

Louie Hanson died in the automobile, slumped sideways against his son with a broken rib through one lung, which would have been fixable a day or so earlier. I went to the funeral but wouldn't look in the coffin.

The men and women in Warner Valley functioned as my family, even if it was only a bunkhouse family, and I want to repay their generosities.

Jake O'Rourke died in the bunkhouse. Jake didn't show for breakfast, and I sent a man to wake him, but he was dead in his bed. I'd like to say that his eyes were otherworldly, and mirrors in which I could see myself, but they weren't like that. Jake's eyes were dry as stones. It was my first not-in-the-coffin confrontation with death.

Vance Beebe came to wheezing, crippling emphysema from a lifetime of smoking and summers of running a hay baler through the clouds of swirling chaff and dust. He couldn't bear to be without cigarettes. Even after he turned a kind of blue color, and was forced to quit smoking, Vance would carry an unopened pack of Pall Malls in his pocket until the cellophane wore out. Then he would throw them away, buy another pack, and carry that, unopened but ready.

There came a time when he couldn't work in the fields anymore. So I told Vance to just sort of retire and loaf in the bunkhouse and fill in where he pleased, but he hated it. One evening he called me aside. "Damn," he said, "I can't stand this life." He looked at me seriously; I can still remember his eyes, flecked with gold. I passed it off as just a way of making talk.

Vance spent that summer building chairs for the bunkhouse bullpen on a design from upstate New York rich man resorts. Then he took his emphysema to town and died alone in a motel, and I thought maybe he killed himself. I still do. Vance believed in doing your own work.

One of my straw bosses worked out his last years as a high school janitor, the best job he could get after he moved to town. That seemed right. I understood the incapacities of the men in my bunkhouse as part of my deal, something to be lived with. I was due some arrogance, I thought, like everybody else.

Lee Mallard ran the combine through three or four harvests. We probably didn't speak a thousand words. Lee didn't talk to anybody; he ran himself as an absolutely single-minded man. He was an artist of working, and I was an immature boss. It was as if Lee Mallard knew a secret—you could make up for all the world's infidelities by doing your work well. He was the grim saint of combine men, and then he died in terror of his oncoming death. All this work, I had to see, had earned him nothing. Or so I thought.

Slim Poore was crippled by his broken back but he went on farming, unable to do more than supervise in a foot-dragging, shuffling fashion. Slim couldn't sign his name and he couldn't quit, because there was no way to escape. Slim was a man with no options save being sustained by his wife and his family.

On the muddy days in the early spring I would see his gray Ford pickup parked on a slippery levee-bank road down by the fields where he farmed. Margaret, his wife, would be out in the wind with a blue paisley scarf tied over her head, laboring at the wheel on some headgate valve. Slim would be clutching at the pickup box with stiff fingers, eyeing the rush of irrigation water.

He would lift his squinty grin to me from under that Ben Hogan golf cap. "Well there, Buckshot," he would say, as if amused both at his predicament and me. Having already run out of excuses for myself, I learned to ignore a man so crippled and willful and actual.

In the evenings I would go home to eat with my wife and our children, the day over to the degree that it is ever over in agriculture. I was free from the fields until morning. I read my secret, intellectual books; I led my other life; such looking away from entrapments and death and its possibilities mostly worked, until it didn't. If I had known anything about my own mind I would've found a way to leave. I would not have waited until everything dissolved into insubstantiality, if that makes any sense, until my actualities drifted away and became (pathologically) a sort of dream or light show. I came to believe reality was nothing backed up by nothing at all.

Not once did I ever talk to Slim Poore about his sudden crippling, or what he thought of a world so absolutely without mercy. Such talk, I imagined, would have embarrassed him; or maybe not, I see now, maybe he would've loved to talk. Once we got started, we might have speculated our way through some philosophies. It would have been a terrific help to me.

Since childhood I have mostly been able to persuade myself that I would not have to confront my own death in any immediate sense until I had figured out how to make peace with that most terrifying of all theoretical possibilities, the worst news in nature, the single time it comes. If someone died I paid only oblique attention, focusing my mind elsewhere. I learned to look away.

My father boozed through some long winters, mostly in a hotel bar called the Ponderosa Room in Klamath Falls, doing hard time and worrying his heart into a series of attacks by the early 1960s. I went to see him in Red Bluff, where he was hospitalized, convinced he was dying, and found him at the jovial center of a little population of men without women who seemed to be counting themselves lucky. He acted as if he was at peace with the idea of dying early. It was somehow reassuring. But he had not given up on anything.

By summer he was back at the Klamath Marsh, where he had grown into manhood and his sister Vi was calling the shots. By this time Bill Gouldin was dead. Warner Valley, where Jack Nicol ruled the roost, was unthinkable. But the Marsh was home. Ada Bolton, who had worked for my mother in Warner, was cooking there. Clyde was dead. She was seeing out her life, and seemed glad for my father's presence. They hovered together amid the isolations over the Klamath Marsh like an old asexual married couple, each supporting the other. Ada cooked my father special meals, and he got quit of the booze. He lost fifty or so pounds, doing some horseback work with the cattle, keeping "on the payroll" as he put it, and nursing himself back to health.

During that time I saw him maybe twice. He was wan and isolated, and as distanced as a man in training. And I think he was. He was getting set for another go at life. Out in the little set of rooms where he lived, most of the things he carried with him were packed in cardboard boxes.

One Fourth of July Pat and Roberta and Janet and I gathered the grandchildren to go visit him, at his invitation, in his old stomping grounds at Odell Lake. He was housekeeping for the summer in the Odell Lake Lodge (there wasn't much left of Millionaires Row down by the creek). He said it was to be a summer of mostly fishing, the retired country man at leisure, spooling away his time, playing out the last good days.

He smiled like it was a terrific plan. But soon you could tell he didn't have any life at all. His favorite bar was a roadhouse on the highway, and the people he sought out seemed to be even more distant from life than he was; I remember a couple of old military men who were discomforted by the presence of his blood relations. The conversations ran to relative merits of various bait, and the intricacies of trolling motors. We fished, we ate out, the children ran frogs in races across the dusty yard outside our rooms. That was it. Odell Lake was not our place to go anymore. I was eager to shake the chill and head for home, where we were in the middle of haying.

What did I owe him? Nothing, that was my notion. He was my father, I was the child, and children don't owe fathers and mothers, not nothing. It was commonplace thinking in our part of the world, and part of our trouble.

My father, I thought, could have told me things to know, actual as a stone with a code engraved on it, a thing you could put in your pocket and carry around, cool and hard and smooth, that you could touch when you were worried. But such a thing was not in our contract.

(My father died since I wrote the early drafts of this material. He was losing his memory. Names, he said, words I want to say, I can think of the words but I can't say them. It's terrible, he said. I never heard him use a word like that before, so seriously, open and vulnerable.)

Every so often, during what some people thought of as his perpetual undergraduate career at the University of Oregon, Pat would run out of money and call me about work. My cousin Jack was cultivating an ever greater remove in his boss-of-the-ranch role, and it was obvious he didn't like the notion of hiring family. But it was understood I couldn't do my job without final say on hiring and firing my own crew, so I told myself to hell with Jack and hired my brother. Later misunderstandings between Jack and me to a large degree proceeded from such twitches of ego. We were territorial in the manner of animals.

Probably hiring Pat was a way of easing myself off the hook for some of the injustices I was taking part in, a way of consoling myself. I could do that much, I told myself, I was okay. Pat had to work hard, I was coldhearted about that, but I was doing the right thing. Maybe the situation was tough on Pat, but that was his fate, the world was tough. "He's got to work," Jack said, "like anybody in the bunkhouse."

The first fall he came back, Pat moved into the little one-room house where Ada and Clyde lived when we were children, and endured the endless clanking monotony of plowing the seven hundred acres in Huston Swamp with our old RD-6. It was sixty days of pumping the grease gun, cranking the starting motor, tasting diesel fumes, climbing into the tight home-built cab, and turning a twelve-foot swath around and around that huge field, eating lunch out of a tin box, studying the horizons and trying to hear yourself think. Once or twice a week I would drive by in my Ford pickup, checking on progress, and wave, and he would wave back, but he never stopped.

As I lie down to sleep on cold nights my imagination can take me out where the Fee Point reaches into the old tulebeds on the east side of Warner, to the shack where my father set up his first grain camp cookhouse, where I watched my mother in that summery wind with that sour-smelling cook named Ida when I was five years old, both of them in yellow cotton dresses, young women on a fine day, gazing out to plowground fields being cut from the swamps.

Close to thirty years later my catskinners crushed that homesteader's house into a pile of weathered junk lumber, dumped on diesel and burned it. It was January and we all warmed our hands on the flames, then turned away to a salamander stove and drank steaming coffee and ate cold roast-beef sandwiches sent out from another cookhouse. The impulse that drove us to such burning was a vision. We were doing God's work, and thought we were making a paradise on earth, a perfection of fields. In hindsight I see so much of that compulsive reordering as absolutely wrongheaded because it precluded reverence or even passing concern for the past. It was such self-absorption that fueled our inability to cherish ourselves and the native actualities of the place where we lived, and it drove our family into trouble.

I don't want these to be the sentimentalities of a man looking back on a lost world from childhood. My boyhood on that ranch was most often a hard, scab-handed affair that often left me yearning for the civilities of my school-year life in town. But in the beginning it was a life conducted on a human scale in a naturally functioning place. Then we began to reshape the place, following a dream of machinelike perfection, a corps of engineers/ag school mirage of remaking the world, and it didn't work any better for practical reasons than it did for spiritual ones.

The ecology of the valley was complex beyond our understanding, and it began to die as we went on manipulating it in ever more frantic ways. As it went dead and empty of the old life it became a place where no one wanted to live. In our right minds we want to seek out places that reek of complexity. Our drive to industrialize soured and undercut the intimacies that drew most people to country life in the first place. God knows, we used to say, nobody but a fool would go into the cow business if he had it in mind to get rich. You'd be a hundred times better off with your money in a string of shoe stores or Dairy Queens. So it is enormously heartening, in recent years, to find signs of backlash.

The old desert cow outfits are refitting their horse-drawn chuck wagons, for economic reasons, so they say, and I'm sure they are right. A four-wheel-drive outfit is going to cost you money right down the line, so many thousands of dollars when it comes shiny new off the lot, and then there are brake linings and drive-line bearings and carburetor kits and broken axles and belted radial tires and all the rest. Horses keep on grass and hay and a shot of oats now and then. And there are other motives for going back to some approximation of the old life. Maybe in the long run these are economic, too. What it comes to is rediscovering reasons for doing the work. Call it the recognition that most of us are eager to live in connection with a specific run of territory and its seasons, in some intimacy with the animals which happen to inhabit that country, creature to creature. We want to live in a living world, and work at significant work like raising food, which as a calling is so unlike the alienating efficiency-dream of agribusiness.

People stick to ranching because they love the feel of a quick little horse moving intently after cattle, or the smell of greasewood after summer rain or new-cut alfalfa on a spring morning, or the stretch of damp rawhide as they work at braiding a riata, or the look of a mother cow as she trails her dusty way back to her calf after a long walk to water. People stick to it because they enjoy the feel and smell and sound of things, and because they share those mostly unspoken loves with other people they can trust as being somewhere near to decent.

All over the American West cowboys and ranchwomen and farmhands and sheepherders have been gathering to declaim their verse to one another. Such gatherings are heartbreaking in their openness once all the hype and nonsense has slipped aside. Like the other side of that bloody-knuckled coin which is rodeo, these are celebrations of things ranchland people respect and care about most deeply—the land they have chosen to live on, their work, and, right at the center, one another, this companionship.

As the economics of ranching deteriorates, our good people seem driven to open themselves. We can all take heart from their willingness to have a try at naming those things they take to be sacred. I think of my mother's piano, the strings popping and twanging in that wreck so many years ago.

Waterbirds were a metaphor for abundance beyond measure in my childhood. On a dour November afternoon my father sat on a wooden case for shotgun shells in the deep tules by Pelican Lake like a crown prince of shotgunning, and dropped 123 ducks for an Elks Club feed. The birds were coming north to water from the grain fields and fighting a stiff headwind. They flared and started to settle, just over him, and they would not stop coming into the long red flame from his shotgun as darkness came down from the east. The dead birds fell, collapsed to the water, and washed back to shore in the wind. Eventually it was too dark to shoot, and the birds were heaped in the back of his pickup and he hauled them to town; he dumped them off to the woman he had hired to do the picking and went on to a good clear-hearted night at the poker table, having discharged a civic duty.

When someone had killed too many birds, their necks were strung together with baler twine and they were hung from spikes in an old crabapple tree back of our house, to freeze and be given away to anyone who might come visiting. While saying good-bye we'd throw in three or four Canada honkers as a leave-taking gift, frozen and stiff as cordwood, and give you the name of the lady in town who did the picking.

What is the crime here? It is not my father's, or not his alone. In later years men came to me and told me he was the finest man they ever worked for, by which, I think, they meant fair and convivial—and, in terms of an implied contract, just. From an old hand who'd worked for room and board, no wages at all, through the Great Depression that was the ultimate praise. They knew he hadn't broken any promises, and they had sense enough to know that finally you can't really help anybody die, no matter how much you owe them. I envy those qualities and wonder at the ease with which I tricked myself into thinking I was trying to make a positive effect in the world, and thus justified in ignoring my father. I deeply regret that our enterprises didn't come to more.

What I really want to do, I think, is retell the stories so they come out with the animals taking care with one another. I wish, for instance, that he'd told me the meat-hunting he grew up with while stalking the early-century flocks of Redheads and green-winged teal and Canada honkers had devolved into something close to ceremonial shot-gunning bullshit by my time. My father knew it, but he didn't say anything; he just quit. Maybe I've spent my life repudiating a style of going at the world he never taught me to understand, and because of that, my father himself. There is always supposed to be such trouble between fathers and sons.

But there was an obvious string of crimes. Maybe we should have realized the world wasn't made for our purposes, that Warner Valley wasn't there to have us come along to drain the swamps and level the peat ground into alfalfa land. No doubt we should have known the waterbirds would quit coming. But we had been given to understand that places we owned were to be used as we saw fit. The birds were part of all that.

What went wrong? Rules of commerce or cowardice or plain

bad thinking? Failure to identify what was most valuable? Did such failures lead me to treat men as if they were no more than tools to be used?

One night in Lakeview I was dancing with a woman we all knew as the crop duster's wife. She came to the taverns every night, beautiful in an overbruised sort of way, but she wouldn't go find a bed with any of us. She was, she claimed, married forever to a man who was off in Arkansas dusting cotton from an old Steerman biwing. She said she just hoped he didn't wreck that Steerman into some Arkansas church and we danced to our music of pleading and powerlessness, please release me, let me go.

We sat at the bar—I was drunk, of course—and I started telling her about Louie Hanson and how he died, and the murderer, and how I sent him back to prison, eager to confess my coldheartedness. Maybe I thought a woman who waited for a man who flew crop-dusting aircraft would understand. Maybe I was hoping she'd fall for a crazy man.

"There is nothing to dislike but the meanness," she said, picking at her words. "You ought to be glad you ever knew those old farts."

Failures of sympathy, she was saying, if I read her correctly, originate in failures of the imagination, which is a betrayal of self. Like so many young men, I could only see myself in the mirror of a woman. Offering the utility of that reflection, and solace, was understood to be the work of women, their old job, to inhabit the house and forgive, at least until they got tired of it.

In those days a woman who wanted to be done with such duties might do something like buy herself a wedding ring, and make up a story about a faraway romantic husband who flew his Steerman every morning to support her. People like me, this woman might say, were no cure for her loneliness. But she might excuse my self-centered sorrowing. She might say we don't have any choice, it's the creature we are. Or she might tell me to wise up and understand that sympathy can be useful only if it moves us to open our hearts.

If you're so taken with stories, she might have said, why don't you imagine a story in which the Murderer does not return to the Oregon State Prison but lives on at the grain camp for years until he has forgiven himself and is healed—a humorous old man you could turn to for sensible advice, a story in which all is forgiven and we have learned to mostly let the birds fly away because meat isn't necessarily what we are hunting.

CHAPTER 7

SLEEPING ALONE

Over the years I have tried to understand that love and not justice is the point of things. But there was an afternoon when I stood on a ditch bank with a dented bucket of luminously orange carrot slices marinated in strychnine, poisoning badgers and dreading every moment I could foresee, and all things were equally unreal: there was my hand in the rubber glove, holding the slice of carrot, which was almost luminous; there were the clouds over Bidwell Mountain; there was my breathing, which was the sound of death in its possibilities all around. There was the possibility of eating a slice of carrot.

I would have to move if I was ever going to get home. Numb with dread and feeling sorry for myself because I felt nothing but terror, I had to know this was craziness. For that condition there is no metaphor; it is precisely like nothing.

By craziness I mean nearly catatonic fearfulness generated by the conviction that nothing you do connects to any other particular thing inside your daily life. Mine was never real craziness, although some fracturing of ice seemed to lie just around the corner of each moment; it was easy to imagine vanishing into complete disorientation. My trouble could be called "paralysis in the face of existential realities," a condition I could name, having read Camus like any boy of my time. But such insight was useless. Nothing was valuable unless it worked toward keeping the lid on my own dis-ease.

On April 11, 1961, a week or so before we would break ground on another twenty-four-hour-a-day swing of farming, I came to suffer what can only be called a breakdown, *things* having turned unreal in a set of quick-time instants while I did my stint of reading in the very early morning before breakfast, an old discipline. If I was going to be a farmer (my logic went) I was not going to give up my reading, even if I had given up my writing (and maybe someday I would be a writer, that file was far from closed). I would do my reading if I had to do it before daybreak, and I did, thinking I was alone in my perseverance, a kind of hero of the hinterlands. But good people all over America do their reading before the work begins. Or at night, to color their dreams.

The most important thing that happened always happens down in the right-hand corner of the frame, as Auden says in "Musée des Beaux Arts," while hardly anyone is watching. In this case it was four-thirty one morning and I was reading *The Magic Mountain* (the perfect text) and a dog, a little beagle puppy, was curled on the couch beside me.

There is a woman in the story who was given to epileptic seizures (we called them fits), and I began to imagine that I was going to dissolve (or die, which is how I saw it) into one myself, right then, there on the couch in my living room. I saw that Guamanian boy from so long ago falling to the muddy ground, down in what I recollected as the demonic green sunlight while we were sweating and chopping bamboo amid the palm fronds. It was going to happen, at any instant.

It was an event I have immortalized for myself (and, having enclosed it in a story, made it harmless for at least a moment). I see it as a little foreshadowing of death (should that instant come when I realize that my body is no longer breathing). That instant of oncoming panic is something I have examined most resolutely. It has become hard with overuse, like a set of baby shoes you have bronzed, to display on the mantel or hang from the rearview mirror. And I have concocted a simple little pathology to explain it as one of those unreal moments you can have when you have lulled yourself into drinking too much coffee in the early morning, when you are for a second able to see into the arbitrary nature of everything. The years are turning but the gears are not meshed. Blame it on caffeine.

You realize the world is meaningless. What foolishness. You shake your head and, you know, the connections come rushing back. Except it didn't work. Nothing came rushing back. Something like a corrosive fog (we could call it terror but it wasn't, it was nothing) began to seep in around the edges of my thinking and fill me until it *was* my thinking, there was no one thinking, there was only a boy grasping at his straws. It was happening; here we go. The time had come.

As it went on happening I stood and took the dozen steps into the bedroom where my wife slept. Each thing in the world was strange and absolutely newborn. The little beagle went with me. My wife breathed her sleep; she was safe, far away in her other country where people were sleeping. I wondered if she could save me, but I didn't say anything because I didn't want anybody to know I was crazy, not yet. Maybe something would happen in just a minute and everything would click back again;

I would not be crazy, and nobody would know anything had happened at all.

The person I most centrally recall from that morning nightmare was an Irish immigrant named Tom McAuliffe, who worked for me as a kind of straw boss, a good decent man. There was a ditch washed out, and I jabbered at him about fixing it, get it fixed, I said, I can't think right now, and he looked at me like maybe he thought I'd been drinking. But he didn't say anything and he got the work done, and I wish he was here, so I could talk to him, and ask him if I acted crazy, a talk for old times' sake, like this writing, but he has been dead a while in Warner Valley, well before his time, where I thought I was vanishing.

A way to typify the quality of the days during that first summer of my difficulty is to say they were *hummers*: they sang with the humming energy of something wrong, not so much evil as dislocation, everything out of joint, like your back can be, as if *things* could be cracked back into alignment. I could almost hear the sun sizzling up there along in its trajectory.

Understand, I thought something in me had probably cracked, but I didn't really think I was crazy. For me, actuality had slipped into nonexistence, call it *unactual*, and yet it wasn't. I never thought the world had gone incoherent. It hadn't dissolved into shadow; it was only incomprehensible. It was there, and would be, I knew it: predictable and yet foreign and unnamed, unnameable. Some incapacitating thing had to be wrong with me—not with the world, not with things. To think the world was wrecked would have been fatal. Too difficult, too lonely.

My only hope, I thought, my eventual fix for all that *wrong-*

ness, was in looking out for Number One. I was correct in considering selfishness as a way of putting a name on yourself, a good idea. But selfishness is also bad and ultimately distancing and doesn't serve the self at all.

I still think it's a smart idea to honor our powers of ego, allowing that they are central to love and the main power we have beyond flat refusal. But I was overwhelmed by notions of freedom and escape. I thought I would never be anyone unless I took care of myself. I forgave myself; infidelities, I rationalized, were often necessary to freedom, and thus political. Our dream of marriage and fidelity, which had looked so seamless, made of bright steel, collapsed before my determination to cherish myself beyond all others.

Driving the levee banks I would grieve for myself and think I had learned too much from books like *The Critique of Pure Reason,* but knowing too much wasn't the trouble. My state of being seemed unspeakable in any language known in my part of the world.

So what I did was go on with the work, watching myself from afar as I walked through my life, driven perfectly batshit by my elevation, floating above a world which was in no way any sort of net. Maybe it wasn't even there so far as I could tell (I still can't tell, but where's the difference?).

In my bed, cold in myself and shaking—like a dog shitting peach pits as we used to say—and wondering what my wife could be thinking about a husband who shook like a dog, I could always sleep, pass out, go to nothing. It was a saving grace, the animal escaping into oblivion. And alone. I wanted to sleep alone; and that says it all. And more.

At last my wife (she was too good, she couldn't stand it anymore was my theory at the time, is still my guess) came to my bed one night and interrupted my shaking. We never talked to each other about whatever it was that had gone haywire in my systems, but she took me out of my brain and that was a kind of reinvention, and I bless her for it, and wish it had really worked. It's easy to think about intimacy as if it was a cure, and to some degree it might be, but our selves are not so fixable. We should have talked, and it was my fault we didn't.

Owen Schwartz was an apprentice cowboy, a boy with the chuck wagon my first summer on the desert. Owen was kind to me. Then he went off to World War II, and my father had the good idea of putting him to farming on shares when he came back, still grinning and willing as a good dog, at least in the beginning. Orphaned in childhood, and diligent to the point of foolishness, he went wrong in his head and died. People let him die. His fate terrified me.

Owen had worked hard and made some money. But when his disguise fell away, he learned to believe that the world owed him some fundamental fairness, allegiance of the kind he was more than willing to return, an expectation which, in an eventual disagreement with that most disagreeable of men, my grandfather, was ruinous. Owen was prideful and foolish enough to give up his acreage when it was obvious the old man wanted him to leave, for financial reasons, thinking my father had made him too good a deal; and, using Owen's pride as a weapon, he drove him off.

By the time I came back to Warner, in the fall of 1957, Owen was trying to make it farming a patch of alkaline land out near the Lakeview airport. He was living poor and alone in a tin shed, and he was angry all the time, always muttering to himself. As it turned out, he was lost forever. Nobody was much surprised when he walked into a physician's office and demanded an operation. He was determined in his belief that someone had embedded wiring in his forearms; he wanted the armature cut out. Having had enough of being controlled by someone else, he wanted to be normal.

Nobody was much surprised when Owen was found dead out by the airport in his tin-roofed shack. No one ever told me what he died of, and, too frightened by his fate, I never asked. He was dead, killed by his craziness, is how I chose to see it. His belief in wires in his arms had been a way of accepting the idea that the moral universe was a trick, a concept he had at least partway learned in his dealings with my grandfather.

Maybe I was going that crazy, and as good as dead. The thought skittered at the edges of my brain. And for a while I was, kind of, except that I didn't let myself dwell an instant on the idea of suicide. *Whoops,* I would think as the notion slipped inside my fences. I would look away to dwell on anything else, anything at all, thinking, *Not today, no sir, not today.* I was a secret. I was a book nobody could read, not even me.

My attention would snap into focus from time to time. On February 20, 1962, John Glenn orbited the earth, and I was full of terror as I drove my muddy roads and worked my water. What if it was me? It could have been. John Glenn was about my age, alive out there so far from anything touchable.

People have always seen patterns in the stars. Like a revolving map over their heads, the configurations in the sky as the earth circled in its perfect cycles were a sure road chart which harmonized with the turn of seasons; there was nothing contingent about them. So it was natural for people to study the heavens as they tried to orient themselves on the surface of the earth.

The night sky was pure overwhelming abstraction, and reminded me too clearly of my isolation. For all of one day in my blue Ford pickup truck, listening to the radio, I could not breathe as I went through the motions of February believing I would die with John Glenn as he circled the earth, if he died out there in nowhere. Our brains, I think, are built to believe in magical connections woven of invisible energies. They are built to spin and weave in lots of ways, too many. It was all too much for me.

What I learned to do was eat little soft pills of vitamin B-12 like they were popcorn. My troubles were strictly chemical; the cure was vitamins. I learned to avoid letting even my thinking venture into places without limits.

I had been taught to pay attention to my own contradictory instructions. Like most of us I'd learned to tell myself to be this and be that, to be both the one thing and the other, to be loved and to be honest, to be sexy and get laid all the time and yet to be desired and true and also anything you want because it's nobody's business but your own, betray them all and know they'll understand deep in their hearts because they are betraying you. Be one and everything at the same time. Until you are nothing.

I took too much philosophy to heart. I loved Immanuel Kant. Still do, I think, in a kind of beguiled way. We can't prove that the world resides in some inherent logic which isn't simply make-believe—that was the idea I loved in the beginning. I thought it explained away God's trickiness. But it broke my heart before I was done.

And then, the good animal, I began to find I had managed a few moments at the beginning of each day before I remembered I was crazy. I would wake up to myself and not even think about my good companion *the panic* until maybe ten minutes had passed and I was already in the shower, or sipping a cup of coffee. I learned to walk on that time as if it was ice, every so often getting out a little farther before the surface sagged and creaked, and the cracks radiated from the place where I stood for another day. But in those days I never had the child's sense to notice that I could look out any pane of glass to the morning and see that the world was alive and up to something, even if I couldn't demand it be anything but what it was.

Over a couple of years of drifting back and forth between Eugene and the ranch, Pat worked up to lead man on the hay-baler crew in the summer, ran a self-propelled combine in the barley harvest, and functioned as straw boss for the catskinners rebuilding the long dike around the outside of the valley in the late fall, all the while drawing regular field-hand wages. His presence was a great steadying thing for me in my dizziness.

Then, in the early summer of 1963, he ran off to Reno and married a stylish, good-looking young divorcée whose parents had bought a ranch out west of Lakeview. Pat, for once, had called his own shot—it was a surprise to all of us. She had a child, and they were suddenly a family. One of the prefab houses we'd put up for married couples was empty, so the newlyweds settled in amid rustic jokes and some partying. I was so determined to find only existential emptiness in the world that I envied what I imagined as their innocence, and was both frantic and condescending.

What I had learned to do was live all the time in disguise, with two lives: one ordinary (or so it seemed) and masterfully enacted (or so I thought), while my other, inner life was absolutely unmoored. And then came a sequence of days which led me to wonder if maybe it wasn't the world that was crazy, after all. Maybe we were all milling animals, and all our philosophies utter horseshit.

In November 1963, Pat and I took our families off to Eugene. This was not an ordinary thing for us to do, not as our lives had worked out by then. It took an effort, I think, on our part, to act ordinary—to go to Eugene, see some people, some football, old friends, something I hadn't tried since that homecoming in Corvallis four years earlier, when I got so drunk in the lobby of the Benson Hotel. But actual history intruded. We were planning to visit my mother and spend the weekend with buddies from our college days; simple and proper, we even had tickets for the Civil War game in Eugene, between the University of Oregon and Oregon State. The Ducks and the Beavers. We were driving north in the autumn sunlight along the shores of Summer Lake when the regular radio broadcast was interrupted by the speculations and the rumors that Kennedy had been shot, confirmation, and then the news our football game had been canceled. We went on anyway.

In my mother's house was an endlessness of television and whiskey, all weekend long. Down in the Eugene VFW Club, a white dance-hall building with pillars where my people eventually located their energies, the knots were untied and the house party was beginning. My wife danced with college boys and looked to be enjoying some ideas. Why not? That *was* the idea. And I suggested to a young wife of some student that we make away for the weekend, and asked my wife if she minded. Some business like that, very drunk, far gone on an idea of the center not holding, and on a getaway.

The killing of John Kennedy was like permission to fuck around, maybe just to fuck. Everybody understood some version of that message. What was the use of caution or circum-

spection or good manners or prudence or good looks if
somebody would shoot you anyway?

This was the beginning of what I have learned to think of
as my false recovery. Detective novels proceed through a series
of so-called false solutions to a real solution. And that is the way
this one works, exactly as those stories are supposed to go. The
first thing to learn was might as well have a drink and lighten
up; and fuck somebody. And that is the false solution, in which
the cure is selfishness.

I went to watch Louie Hanson's funeral and thought anything possible was a false solution of some sort or another,
and frightened myself into putting such thoughts far away. So,
selfishness.

Looking back, I seem to have been so soft and easily wounded.
By which I mean fundamentally untouched. Janet and I didn't
see much of the world outside eastern Oregon, except on television, and then only one channel and not a good one. For years
I endured the afternoon idiocies of the American Football League
while the NFL was playing on stations we didn't get. We watched
a dim version of the Beatles in their first televised extravaganza.

I was confirmed in my notion that things had gone on without me. Maybe they had always been different than I thought.
Maybe whatever's real is always a trick. Maybe that is something everybody believes in some part of their thinking. It might
just be that the colorful world is a deception, a joke. Out in
Warner Valley we laughed about hippies and the beginnings of
Haight-Ashbury. But nobody went south to check out the actualities. We had television if we were hungering for news from
what we were coming to think of as the Visible World, which
we hated for its self-importance when all the time it was maybe

only something to do. And then came a night in which every-thing was transformed. Birds woke us, the nights were soft, sun-light lingered into evening over the rims to the west, and I was healing, or so I hoped without much believing, but our house was never whole again.

On the north edge of Lakeview there is a motel and night-spot built around a swimming pool fed by natural hot springs. In those days it was called Hunter's Hot Springs Lodge, and nicknamed Hunter's Hot Lodge. On July 3, 1963, I stopped in for a drink before heading home through the soft twilight, and there was Ross Dollarhide's son.

Rossie, we called him, a certified hero (World Champion Steer Wrestler, 1953) and out of my childhood to boot, drinking and looking for company, some talk about old times. Rossie was a huge, attractive man who treated life as if it had to be burned up each day, before it got away. He was crippled by a leg which had been broken over and again until it refused to heal, and wore a stainless steel brace down the outside of his right boot. Lately he'd been playing Indian in the movies, his body painted red, horseback and shirtless, and making Chrysler commercials. He never got to speak, but got off the train looking like the cowboy any rich woman would want to get into her Imperial or New Yorker.

People moved to be near him. I still find men who talk about Rossie as if things sort of stopped being so interesting for a little while after he died. That night he was lonesome, I think. He acted as if he'd been looking specifically for me, as if he and I were the only adults in sight—men together—and I was a some-body of consequence and not a man who'd never got past work-ing for his own family. So I was hooked.

A woman named Tootie Gunderson was tending bar. An Indian rodeo hand named Beef Miller was trouble as soon as he

showed up with his brothers. "Dollarhide," he said. The fighting
that soon enough got under way was a natural culmination of
hostilities having to do with the history of racism in rodeo. This
was a world where people acted out their passions and worried
about it later, so we all headed out to the parking lot. They
beat each other bloody, two huge sweating men who would not
collapse. I was so drunk I could barely see them in my mind's
eye the next morning when I woke up in my pickup truck. The
luminous day had begun, the sun rising in my eyes. I was miles
from Warner Valley, in the parking lot outside Hunter's Hot
Lodge, and I was missing breakfast with the men in the grain
camp cookhouse. This had never happened before. If the men
working for me ever pulled a stunt like that, they were auto-
matically fired. Those were the rules.

But them who makes the rules gets to break them. That was
my logic as I rubbed my eyes and remembered the night: Fuck
the rules. I had already begun suspecting there was something
useful in the concept of release into therapeutic drunkenness,
and that night with Rossie the notion got coupled with the vir-
tues of heedlessness. In the theory of life I was closing in on,
selfishness was pure and necessary. It became an excuse for
whatever you wanted to do. I was still drunk, and anyway, we
were starting a holiday, who would really know? I could fake
it. And that was another part of fucking the rules: You can
fake it.

But not later in that long day, which had been set up as a
family day. Jack Nicol and Maryann and Janet and I were driving out to a little hideout with all our kids, a desert horse-raising
ranch we owned just over the border into northern Nevada.
The women were bringing food, and we were going to lay out
our spread on the grass by the sweet creek. We were family
and in theory, friends. But Jack was turning into a long-jawed,

impatient, cigar-smoking man. Likely his frustrations ran as deep as mine, but we didn't talk, and soon we were into an arrangement in which our friendship was increasingly distant, and doomed. Jack was the majority stockholder, boss of the ranch, and he demanded that his authority be absolute. I was beginning to resent him, inventing reasons why I should be willing to play tricks on him along with everybody else, and increasingly willing to play the fool myself. Which is probably, as we know, a form of pathology.

Jack had it in mind to rebuild an irrigation dam that had been washed out since the 1920s. That was the idea, planning the job. Except that by afternoon I was deeply chemical, lost in a hallucinatory hangover, and puking out my side of the pickup when I thought nobody was looking except for Janet and the kids, who were bound with me in my deceptions, regarding me with curious solemnity, as if they were witnessing something not so much disgusting as sort of interesting and somehow connected to the real and glamorous cowboy past of Rossie Dollarhide in his ancient glory. The rumored world of my childhood.

This, for a good boy like me, was a nightmare, but it was also actual—an illness caused by something real. It sure beat weightlessness, and actually felt like a cure; the night before, I had been drunk and thoughtless, and for a while I'd cut loose of my anxieties. So now I was sick, and maybe still a little bit out of myself. It was possible to imagine I had found a secret tunnel into the actual world. Just for a little while, I thought, I'll be like this as long as it takes to heal, then I'll turn back. I was a crazy man. Janet and I looked at one another, our eyes met. She forgave me. I was learning a technique. Every minute of that day was a betrayal.

Not long afterward I sat at the bar in that dark barroom in Lakeview called The Indian Village, eyeing their Indian arrowheads, many of them no doubt from Warner Valley, chipped from black obsidian, which were displayed in heart-shaped and other arrangements, mounted on white cotton batting, framed alongside the mirrors. I was seriously tired of my battle with the self, and I drank and talked in a simple fashion with some men who happened to come into the bar. Then I thought I should drive home over the Warner Mountains to Adel.

I went a few blocks, then pulled into the shadows behind the Safeway and sat there sipping a can of beer and listening to Patsy Cline on the car radio, pleased that I had forgotten my troubles for a while. I was drunk again, and felt closer to okay than I had in years. I had never been so happy, nor so frightened. First I was the good simple boy, then I was a crazy man, and now I was the fellow standing over the abyss who had discovered he could be at ease with himself when he was drunk. I was flat hysterical with release, whistling along with "trailer for sale or let" (Roger Miller). Good and drunk. And in these country taverns it seemed there were other people like me, scared to death by the unreality of things. We knew, and shared the silences as furtively as cats.

I could drink and turn untouchable. To leave on the outbound train for freedom, connected to no one and invisible, something had to be sacrificed—trust, for instance—if I was going to make my journey alone. The constraints of family came to stand for entrapment; booze and roundhouse fucking all over town represented escape. Survival and infidelity looked like sides of the same coin.

The summer twilight had gone luminous. It was August of that summer and my children were dark figures on the concrete irrigation dam, silhouetted against that light. The water between us was curling with places where fish might live. As darkness came down I went on fishing without knowing how much it mattered, the moment in which that was all I was doing. Then we went home and sat at our table and I looked across to my wife and had a drink of whiskey. I can taste that whiskey.

It is not my business to know what Janet thought. I cannot know. We argued in traditional ways. She was angry and felt grievously betrayed, but she conducted herself with dignity. She was also humane. She tried to understand what was wrong, she tried to help, but she couldn't. I wouldn't let her. My terrors were my secret, and so were my cures, and not to be discussed. To admit that I needed help was beyond me.

There was a married woman who came back from Portland saying she'd been up there "acting as a professional prostitute." She was playing the hard-eyed woman. "He still loves me," she said out of the side of her mouth, talking with what I took to be contempt about her husband, the saw-filer. "At least he says he does." I said you had to wonder. It was almost Christmas, and she'd come home from her wars in a belted, stylish Portland raincoat, a plain hawk-faced woman who had come to what I understood as a true recognition about her life in southeastern Oregon. She had been crazy for something to happen; she'd yearned to risk her life for a new batch of possibilities. She looked her craziness in the eye and went to Portland.

I admired her courage and told her so, as a way of winning her attention, so she consorted with me. Maybe I was the only person in town who would pay her any attention. I was in the bars, it was a dull winter, and I was out and about night after night, snooping. I liked her because she was there to like. One night we shared a motel room for a couple of hours, and after we were through with each other she told me, "No more.

He says he'll kill himself if I don't cut it out. It's true. Why wouldn't he?"

It made sense. We were living in desperate days, getting through them one at a time, hanging on as if we were getting better. That was the story I was living out. I forgave myself, I sorrowed for her husband, and I despised my complicity in what I took to be her cruelties. Now I can see that she only wanted to be like me, as she thought I was: propertied, and betraying, unfettered. I wanted to be like her husband, innocent and decent, honest and betrayed. Even all the while I was taking comfort in his powerlessness, which no doubt made my own look less extreme, I wanted to defend him.

I suppose I flirted with what I regarded as the sad working classes because they seemed so *decent*, as opposed to the impure self-consciousness that was central in my own overbookish disease. Maybe those people were dumb and therefore okay. Maybe I thought those men and women were apt to be as broken as I was, but resolute and stoic about it, and enduring. But I wonder if I was ever so stupid; certainly I hope my thinking was somewhat more complex.

On the dance floor in The Indian Village one night, I got myself blindsided by a sucker punch which took me out for a moment or so. Put me down. When I came conscious I was sitting there on the floor—nobody paying me much attention because the woman I'd been dancing with was putting on some colorful hysterics. The purple ribbon on her cowgirl hat was trailing down the middle of her back as she stood with her fists clenched and the veins standing out on her neck, baying at the stucco ceiling in a shrill voice that drowned the three-piece band into numb astonished silence. With her eyeballs tipped back in her head until there was nothing to see but the whites she was shrieking for God to save her from this fucking *shit*.

The young man who'd punched me, her husband, was staring at her as if he'd just then come to his own personal discovery of sadness—the collapse of his first marriage as it happened—opening and closing his fists and grasping at nothing.

When a few of the women had calmed her down, hustling her out of there to finish the night in another bar, the husband came over and offered to buy me a drink. I can't remember his name, but I took the drink. "Goddamn it," he said. "You know."

Sure enough, I did, at least in my imagination, but I wasn't going to let him off that easy. "There was nothing going on," I said, ignoring my hopes that there soon enough would have been. Something like the sadness of waking up in a motel room with his wife. "She's been drinking three days," he said. "Night before last she was down in New Pine Creek all night. So she's drinking tonight, because she feels so bad about it.

"There ain't no kids," he said. "Well, shit." And now he was grinning. "You couldn't expect me to hit *her*." Endurance, I should've seen right then and so many other times, has more to do with humor than with anything resolute or stoic. But mostly I didn't see, not in any useful way. I understood that I was wounded, suffering from a fall in which I had lost track of reasons why one thing was more significant than another. I was driven to anesthetize myself with selfishness. For years I saw booze as a fence against my fear that nothing was real, and sex as a doorway into something that might turn out to be.

The flashy, roving men who bought cattle had always functioned as prime liberated spirits on our edge of the West; it was their role to bring the money and make the deals. They were men on the move in big cars, living in motels, a pocketful of folding cash, wide hats, Rolex watches, and championship calf-roping buckles from their rodeo days. They would arrive in the early fall, missionaries from a state of mind in which all things, including money, were possible, and nothing, not even money, was to be taken seriously.

They, I thought, would bear some scrutiny. At once gracious and selfish, they knew the true worth of things; they had no homes, they lived nowhere we knew, they dealt in abstractions such as cows to be shipped and money to be banked. Nothing they touched was real, and they knew it. They dealt in essences.

Ours was a deeply two-hearted way of life, tied on the one hand to country and its isolations and seasons and animals, and on the other to town and money and numbers. Except for bankers and their roving bad boys, the cow buyers, few of us really understood the latter. The cow buyers also knew never to put their money on justice, and thus they were to be feared, like saints; and they knew it. In their cynical, grinning, boyish death's-head way, they knew the true worth of things. It is easy to make fun of such men, but they were not fools.

I watched them, looking for clues. I was convinced that I was missing my life, and that it would be a sin, actually, to die cautious, which is to say, so dumb. I admired and envied, for instance, the wit of a friend who bought a full-scale logging truck and used it for nothing but picking up his mail. "It's like a disguise," he said. "People get so upset about your logging truck they never notice what you're really doing."

Renounce middle-class ambition, that was my notion, and I was ready, in town and edgy on long afternoons. On such occasions, techniques for self-discovery were not only life's tools, they were ways of cultivating a bad boy's dream. The beauty of afternoon light touches and dignifies each mote on the scuffed dusty floors of old barrooms. Our shabbiest stumbling impulses from deep in the heart of the previous night turn luminous as we tell stories and laugh and get into the sauce again. This barroom life, we know, is funny and human and fragile and glorious, or at least just as all right as staying home. Or so I thought.

There is no recalling the name of the particular livestock merchant who led me through the adventures that began in the light of a particular afternoon. But I can see his face, a raffish man who would travel on a handshake, two or three clean shirts, some traveler's checks, and a reputation for getting back to you with the money. He was sitting at the bar with some friends, and they were laughing as if nothing in the world had ever been worse than a little bit foolish, and I watched them from the corner of my eye, jealous of their ease but too standoffish and frightened to attempt joining them. There was no such thing as easy familiarity, not for me, until we were maybe an hour or so into the drinking, which in the old days meant five or six quick glasses of Cutty Sark and soda, after which anything we could think of was something we ought to do.

Drinking my way into the action was a trick I had already mastered. So I was eyeing the cow buyer and his friends as potential co-conspirators. But the real center of attention that afternoon in The Indian Village was across the empty dance floor. A couple of Lake County businessmen were entertaining the women who'd come up from Reno to be their weekend guests. In short, in the words of the cow buyer, as he grinned at me and acknowledged my thanks for buying a round, "a couple of *whooors.*" He drew the word out as if he was an owl and he was hooting.

These women were thirtyish and tight-jawed, and looked to be tired of their weekend with these fat old men who were paying the freight. They were lean and would've been handsome by our standards had they got themselves up differently. But on that afternoon in Lakeview they seemed to be dressed to advertise their continuation of some unspoken deal with humiliation.

One of them was short, a little more stylishly built than the other, maybe a year or two older, but in this memory of dancing with them in the afternoon light of The Indian Village they look interchangeable. Maybe it was the eye makeup, the net stockings, and the leather-like skirts, which were constantly working up to something dark and unseeable at the crotch. Me and the cow buyer were game for an afternoon, and we were having one dance after the other, and the men they'd come with were sitting there on the far side of the dance floor with nothing to do but watch, and it wasn't funny. Then one of them called out that it was time to go.

Me and that cow buyer were playing the jukebox and circling on the dance floor, I was smelling dangerous perfume, paired up with the younger woman, the heftier one, the quiet, softer one, some might say the dumb one, except she turned out to be smarter than me. Those potbellied businessmen were watching while we stole their dates, and we hadn't given them any way to save face. Me and the cow buyer and the so-called *whooors* were conspiring to embarrass them. I knew that much, and I would learn some more things.

I was glad to be included. The cow buyer was buying all the drinks. "Shit, kid," he said, "save your money." He was at most only five years older than me, but I was the kid. I knew it was true. He understood the way of things, and I didn't.

Anyway, to hell with those men. They had their weekend, however it was, and to hell with people in general, and their bullshit rules. Nobody cares was a program I could subscribe to without much difficulty or thought. *Fuck 'em all and sleep till noon* was a theme song people were learning to admire all over

America. A revolution was taking shape, and we were part of it without even knowing it. We were just some outlandish boys in The Indian Village in Lakeview, Oregon, on the afternoon after the Labor Day Rodeo was finished, when all but a few of us were gone back to the ranch, to the job. Such was the romance.

I cannot tell you how much I admired the cow buyer when he stepped away from his dance companion and went over to stand looking down on those fellows at their table, displaying his smile like a quick show of cards. "You fellows might as well go on," he said.

"Maybe we won't," one of them said.

"Maybe I'll kick your ass." The cow buyer was still grinning, his face shining with a little whiskey sweat and his hat pushed back on his head in the fashion of a schoolyard bully. The fat men scooted around from behind the table and made their way across the empty dance floor, outside into the light, leaving us to it.

From midafternoon the action is confused for a long time, until well past dark. The four of us, me and the cow buyer and those women, we were paired up in two double beds in the only motel room available for the night at the famous Hunter's Hot Lodge on the northern edge of Lakeview. The man who rented us the room was somebody we knew. From the start he didn't like our action, but what the hell, I thought, it was a story he could tell at the barber shop.

What I recall is making love in a quick way. Not furtive, scurrying, or brutal, but quick. And isolated, more than anything; isolated, and actually alone. It was over and they were still making love in the other bed, making noises like snuffling animals on the other side of a waist-high partition. It was surprising to me that my leader, the cow buyer, would sound so childlike at anything. This was not simple fucking they were at over there. My woman on her back was gazing at the dim ceiling as if visions were playing across the cheap tiles. My isolation in that sagging bed intensified. So I put on my clothes and I went down to the large deserted barroom, where I imagined I would be a cock of the walk and deeply admired as I ordered my scotch and soda. When I looked around, nobody was paying attention, and I was back where I'd started the afternoon, alone at some bar, and deeply chilled in my being. Another run at things was over. It would lead to going home in the deep hours of night, denying guilt. It was nothing new, I saw that in my self-pity, just more of everything.

Back in our motel room, I was surprised and, at first, deeply offended. The women had changed beds. My friend the show-boating cow buyer was energetically bedding the woman who'd been in my bed. They did not appear to notice the quiet opening and closing of the door. The other, the older of those women, and someone truly good in my book of memory—she was in my bed. In the flickering orange and blue light of reflected neon I could see her eyes as she lifted a hand to me. "Come on," she said, and I had enough sense to get out of my clothes and under the covers with her. I don't remember the sounds of anything other than her whispering.

"Slow down," she said, or something like that, and she started teaching me to breathe slowly, touching me everywhere in a feathery way as she did, calming my hands, persuading me that it was my duty to lie back, at least for this moment while I was learning from scratch.

What she was teaching was what we all should have learned, us boys out West, since those days. I learned that my woman in the next bed with the cow buyer had got damned little satisfaction from my thirty-five-second poke, and that was why she had moved on. She didn't owe me anything, and if I wanted allegiance I'd better learn to slow down and attend to the rewarding of someone, as someone right then was attending to me. I was learning that this dynamic is at the heart of everything. I was learning that we should touch one another, and go out into the world smelling and tasting. I learned that I was willing, like anybody would be if they'd let themselves, once somebody told me what was what. Since then I have learned to my sadness that none of this will ever come instinctively, for reasons which likely have a lot to do with my upbringing.

But that is not the point: the point is the woman, and her anxious look as she began with me, whispering and touching, as if she was not at all certain I would be able to get beyond myself and understand anything at all, and her delight as I came easing around my distant bend into willingness, and the way her confidence grew and warmed. What I mostly recall are her attempts at perfection as she made her gifts to me. It is not, as she pointed out, something to get on with, it is the most important part of what there is.

By this time the cow buyer and the other woman were finished and they were listening and that was all right too. What we were doing felt like truth, and you had to be trusting. I didn't mind anyone listening as long as that good woman went on whispering to me and each smell and the look of her hair on the white pillow in the dim light and each movement was precisely as it should be.

And then the man who ran the motel banged on the door to run us off. "You and them whores," he shouted. This was a respectable motel, and there was going to be police and general scandal if we weren't out of there in ten minutes.

And we were. Even the cow buyer in his wide experience with power and money was terrified, so we banged around in that motel room, getting into our clothes, stomping into our boots. We buckled our buckles as the women made a pass at combing their matted hair.

There was no scandal. But for months afterward, unable to connect, deep in the night, I would console myself with the idea that everything I wanted might be "in the wind" if I would only slow down. Not that I did. It was not possible, in such a head-long place as the working man frontiers of southeastern Oregon and northern Nevada, at least for someone so crippled in his balance as me. I was not fit to bring about any revolutions in style. Maybe I told myself something like that.

Anyway, I never said a word about such secrets to a soul. It was months before I saw the cow buyer again. We just grinned and never spoke, but we knew. I thought maybe everybody had always known, that it was only me who had to be taught.

Life in Lake County, Oregon, as I came to engage it, did not involve much in the way of pacing. There were, as always, many of us seeking after excess and dislocation of the sensibilities. I was deeply interested in distracting myself from my own fearfulness of what I saw and sometimes still see, which is that all things are really not connected in any visible or understandable way.

Once upon a time another cow buyer and I found ourselves swimming in the steaming pool at Hunter's Hot Springs while snow fell from a dark midafternoon November sky. It was just the two of us and the handsome woman who ran the place, and a much younger woman, more vaguely formed, who might have been her daughter. And the world lay before us, and then we were too drunk. I woke up in one of the little rooms, where the daughter lived with her pair of sad-eyed children. This, I thought in my craziness, is something I will set right. I will lead this poor girl back to the world.

And crown her the queen of the May, I guess. I talked her into dressing up in her fanciest glitter and making up her eyes with mascara and eyeliner—the whole nine yards—and took her uptown to The Indian Village, where at midnight we were going to begin our new life. She was almost a child herself, but working hard at duplicity. I don't know what she thought except that she was willing to give it a try.

An older woman, known to everyone in that world, stopped me at the door to the bar. "You get her the hell out of here," she said. "Your father's in there." I glanced around a corner and there he was, across the dance floor, at a table with the good woman who would become his second wife.

CHAPTER 8

SELLING OUT

E arly in the 1960s, in solemn conclave, my family voted to sell the ranch in Warner Valley. Getting the job done took six or seven years.

Ours was what is called a third-generation family, shirtsleeves to shirtsleeves. The old man, it is said, talking about my grandfather, he got his name on that property, it's the best ranching property in the West, and now them grandkids will piss it away. Count on it.

The folk talk was accurate, not that it took any genius to foresee that future. Most of my grandfather's grandchildren wanted out, for reasons having to do with money and power, which in the end is the same as possibility. If we were going to find our own lives, it was time to get started, and we knew it.

What we owned was not land, but shares in the Warner Valley Livestock Company. The company did not, as policy, pay dividends. Profits went back into the property. Which was a pretty good deal if you were a majority stockholder with tax problems. But not so hot for minority stockholders who might want to invest their own money. Or squander it on racehorses or trips to Tibet.

What the Warner Valley Livestock Company paid was salaries. If you worked for the company, you got a salary; if not, as they say, you didn't get shit. So it came to pass that some family members, like my sister, who were unlikely ever to be employed in the ranching business, decided they'd rather spend it on frivolities if they damn well pleased. I like to suppose the outcome might have been different if each of us had owned some land individually, real acres we could walk on and dig holes in. We might've felt ourselves connected to pretty things like the ring-necked Manchurian pheasants nesting down next to the sloughs in the Thompson Field, or found ourselves attached to one particular place, if only in our imaginations. We might have talked about this place, such talk being a powerful aphrodisiac and way of holding people to the soil.

At family gatherings the desire for some immediate cash was considered cheap, and shortsighted foolishness. Since I was one of the few getting a salary, it took me a while to realize that my lot was with the heretics. I wanted out. People ask me if I don't sometimes wish I was back on the ranch. The answer is no, and always will be. I have a new life, which is mine. I invented it. That other life belonged to somebody else, to somebody's son or grandson.

But when it became likely, early in 1967, that we were at last going to be able to sell the property, I had no coherent idea of what to do next. I always imagined myself as a writer, however failed; I knew that much, and nothing else. We would have some money, and time. We would think of something. But we didn't. We had moved to the north side of Lakeview—for the schools, we said, although I'm sure people on the ranch were justifiably pleased to see me gone. Officially, my daughter was in junior high and it was either move to town or board her out with some family.

Alongside the house there was a one-room study, a remodeled garage with a fireplace where I built smoky fires. Thinking this must be the way writers got it done, in rooms like this, I set up my typewriter. Each morning I was supposed to be going out to the ranch and making at least a pretense of working, though I seldom went. If anybody asked, I told myself, I'd say I was working on my writing. Meanwhile what I was doing was wondering who I might be if I ever came back to myself, finally facing the idea that if I was not a writer, then I was nothing.

Writing was my only purpose, I told myself, and I worked hard at this, my main chance in life. I wrote and rewrote, before breakfast and after dinner, hung over or not, but I mostly couldn't understand my own stories. My life was luminous with significances I couldn't see. My wife clerked in a drugstore. We looked at houses in Klamath Falls. We thought about buying one once the ranch was sold. No one knew what we would do in Klamath Falls, but maybe we would live there. I pictured a study with creamy white paint and small-paned French windows looking out on a garden and the town below.

I was hanging on, obsessed by my sense that most people knew a secret; maybe it was imprinted in their genes, or else something they had been told by their mothers, but it was nevertheless one secret more than I knew. All I knew were my own confusions. My condition must have been visible to anyone who wanted to see. People turned their eyes away. My son played Little League, and my daughter had a date. Why couldn't I pay attention, back when we were there together, to anything actual?

Maybe because I was more interested in the woman who called on the telephone every day or so. She read part-time as a fiction editor at a literary magazine, and the talk drifted from literature to sex. I called her back. She was, I think, as lost and crazy as I was, reaching as we all sometimes do into detailed and risqué conversation. I fell deep into fantasy and spent half my nights on hide-away drunks.

Then, in June, Jack Nicol broke in to my fantasies and sent me off to help with baling hay on the meadows at the River Ranch, on the Ana River north of Summer Lake, the first property my grandfather ever bought, back in 1911. By this time, Jack and I were scarcely able to speak to each other, close to totally alienated, each unable and unwilling to make sense of the other. I had given up on any pretense of meaningful work, and he was absorbed with planning the future of his properties. He gave the orders, and though I hated him for it there was nothing I could do. I'd sold out to his authority a long time before, so I threw a few things in my Jeep pickup and headed for the River Ranch.

The hay crew lived in an old motel by the highway. Winter Rim, named by John C. Frémont in 1847, loomed at our backs as we gazed over the long reach of twilight across the alkali flats. The days were hot and long, a delirium. I did not call home. Every evening I would stand in the booth in the motel parking lot and call my literary woman; we talked sex, we got right down. This was the life, I thought, because it was based on perfect candor.

Then I went home for the Fourth of July, and found a North American Van Lines truck parked in the street outside the house where I had lived like a prince of irresponsibility. Men were loading furniture; Janet was leaving me. I was thirty-five years old, my boyhood finished. I was enormously, foolishly, surprised. And deeply frightened. We can die of isolation. I thought I might be, and tried to find a couple of women, but—no surprise, this—they were not talking to me. So I rode out drunk into the dying afternoon. I wept and tried to see beyond my baby-boy sort of terror. *So these are the consequences.*

It was important to head my life in the direction of significance. I ran from my wreckage, back to the River Ranch, and on to the Klamath Marsh, insinuating myself into the pity of my aunt, Vi Gouldin, and Sue and Glenn Tingley, relatives who were really strangers. They were kind to me in an offhanded way. And I began to ease my way toward a guarded friendship with my brother, Pat. We were equals for the first time in our lives, a pair of boys working out the summer, waiting for the ranch to sell, wondering what to do now. He was married and I wasn't, but other than that we were in the same box. In the fall of 1965 Pat had quit Warner and moved his wife and child to student housing in Eugene, to finish up a degree in philosophy at the University of Oregon. "But I was never smart enough," he said. "I'd sit in those classes in mathematical logic, and figure I was about ten IQ points from first rate." So he abandoned the idea of graduate school, and went back to work as a ranch hand at the Marsh, driving seventy miles from Klamath Falls every day, working his hours, and keeping his mouth shut and his nose clean, a good boy, waiting for the ranch to sell. I suspect my father steered him away from Warner and working for Jack.

So Pat was the responsible brother, and I was the ne'er-do-well, living alone in the sprawling brick house Vi had built on the point above the Williamson River when my grandfather's house burned down in 1949, eating an occasional meal in the cookhouse across the way. But mostly I was running a baler, drinking my nutrition, driving the pumice-dust roads in the night, across the marshes to the state highway and the crossroad taverns, and trying to ignore my useless freedom.

When I went back to Lakeview there was nothing in the house but books and a few ashtrays. The spaces echoed; it was mine. An old friend came to help me box the books. "Jesus Christ," he said. "You'd be a smart son of a bitch if you read all of these."

Who had I led him to believe I was? Even my friends did not know me in my concealments. My mother and father and my brother and sister and my wife and my children were far away in other lives, and I had better get my ass on the road. I loaded those boxes of books in an old horse trailer and hauled them off to storage, explaining to myself I'd be back for them soon.

In August I went up to Eugene to visit Al, my grandfather on my mother's side, looking for love, as they say. He was the person, I think, who gave himself to me with the most absolute generosity. When I was a child he valued me in a simple way that helped me learn to value myself—the strongest and most useful thing anybody ever gave me. It had lasted all my life, and I knew it still would even when he was dying in an old folks' home and I didn't have any idea how to repay him. In the silence of his room we listened while an old woman down the hall told a sweet childhood story of her own, something about a screen door and a dog and apples on the ground in the orchard, and then told it again, word for word.

"Sweet Jesus. Ixnay," Al said, reverting to our old game of pig Latin. He shook his head as if there was a loose bone in his ear and he couldn't live unless he heard it rattle every so often. He passed one of his broken hands over his eyes at the same time, his fingers thick and the softened calluses still traced with cracks from a lifetime of blacksmithing. For all the years I was a child Al got up early and cooked his own hot cereal, then went to build the fires in the California/Oregon Power Company shop by six in the morning. Some of it, I'm sure, had to do with his need for quiet and isolation before his long day of hammering hot metal, but mostly, I think, he was escaping my grandmother, a woman driven to detailed talk about everyone's afflictions. Running away had become a habit too soon in his life, was what my grandmother said, that and the men he worked with. I think she was glad to see him out of the house, and glad to see him home when he came off shift in the early afternoon, ready to work a couple of hours unmolested in his immaculate garden.

But now my grandmother was dead, and I was sitting with Al in an old folks' home, wanting a drink and imagining the dark bar top, a sweating glass and my cigarettes and a few dollars in change all neatly displayed like a table setting with the back bar and the mirror beyond, where I could study myself anytime I wanted.

A couple of weeks later Al was dead. I never saw him again. When I got to his funeral the casket was closed. It's a quick story. When he died I was in the Eugene Hotel with a thin woman who loved poetry, quoting Denise Levertov (*"it is all a jubilance . . . broken fruitrinds shine in the gutter"*). She made me sad because she wanted things nobody could ever give her, making me feel like a fraud and a failure. There was no fuck like the one she wanted, ever on earth. So I made my excuses, and drove a hundred and fifty miles east across the Cascades to the Klamath Marsh and the empty house and suffered my way into the inevitable hangover, and then the telephone rang on the empty kitchen counter and I found out people had been looking for me the last three days.

Al was going to be buried the next morning. As I drove back to Eugene my solace was the idea that Al wouldn't have done anything but smile at my consternation. But on the way back to the Klamath Marsh I couldn't even hold a conversation with myself.

Every so often I make a run at naming the moment when I came to understand I was becoming someone else. But there was no moment, just a long series of evasions. What I did was mostly instinctual. What saved me was luck.

In late August I had the good fortune to fall into a conspiracy of heartbroken souls with the vivid woman who shared my second marriage. It began on an evening when I tried to write a couple of long letters. It seemed important to keep myself at that kitchen table while the twilight deepened, typing and trying to make sense without thinking about myself. Soon I gave it up and ran to the taverns.

In the late twilight, driving through the swamps, I happened upon a Ford convertible blocking the middle of the road, its top down. Patricia was drunk at the wheel—studying the look of the night, so she said—a tall suntanned blonde wearing an orange bikini. Her feet were smudged, and she reeked of thick perfume like a girl who'd been drinking in that bikini for a couple of days. Like someone experiencing trouble. Like me. She offered me a shot from her bottle of vodka, with a beer chaser, and invited me to a party coming up in a couple of nights, to celebrate the birthday of a local rancher.

It turned out she was living with her father at a place the locals called the Dinosaur Ranch, an attraction designed to draw tourists off the highway between Bend and Klamath Falls. Out in the jack pines nobody cared about life-size plaster dinosaurs. Her father had gone through a stroke, and the hick-town rumors held that he was crazy. I wondered if she was, and sort of hoped so. I was looking for someone to run with, and loved the idea that it might be this handsome woman. "Tomorrow," she said, "I'm going to Silver Lake for booze." She grinned. "I'll leave you a bottle on my way back."

So we sat there in her convertible in that oncoming night. As the last sunlight illuminates the vapor trails of jet airplanes, from almost anywhere out on the Klamath Marsh you can see west to a series of isolated peaks which stand dark along the spine of the Cascade Mountains and then, after night has come down, you can see the snowfields glowing under summer light from the moon. If you knew you were a fool and didn't know how to live, it is something to see that would break your heart.

We talked some addled philosophy, and I decided she wasn't crazy at all. Maybe I was the crazy one, I told her, for trying to believe my life was going to amount to something now that I was free to drink vodka all night long and wake up to find nobody cared. I mean, I said, you have to be tough.

Her bottle was soon empty and we drove to the brick house for more. By this time we were very drunk, but we were talking like children lost in the big woods, and there was no hint of laying hands on each other. We were fast friends, but there would be no pleasures of the flesh, not this time around. This was 1967 and the world was changing; strangers could be friends, just like this. Then she drove away.

The next afternoon, when I came in dusty from the hayfields, a fresh bottle of hundred-proof vodka was sitting on the drainboard in the kitchen in the brick house. Missing one shot. Which was like a message that said, Come join me. Before long I did.

When the haying was over, all the hired people left and the Marsh went empty. I had done my last baling. A man named Clinton Basey and his wife, Mary Ann, were moving into the big brick house. Vi had hired them to look after her acreage on the Marsh, and as she knew, she couldn't have done better. They had worked for years under Bill Gouldin, who had come up under my grandfather. As I understand things, they represent the right-minded side of all my grandfather stood for in his young-man beginnings out on the sagebrush deserts near Silver Lake, before he got it in his mind to assemble an empire. Vi and Mary Ann and Clinton Basey and people like them were hard and decent, survivors in a difficult place, and justifiably proud of themselves.

Pat and I were staying on, at least in theory, to look after my father's interests. In actuality we didn't much know how to look after. When it came time to move cattle or any other serious matter, we followed Clinton. But first I had to move, and I took a four-room house where the ranch mechanic had lived with his wife and three or four kids. It was above the sodded banks of the little Williamson River, surrounded by great yellow-barked ponderosas that sighed in the wind, and filthy. Vi came up from her place on Klamath Lake to help. Horrified by the stench in the kitchen, she laughed and named my new home the Hog House, then went to work, more than sixty years old and a certifiable queen of the country, down on her knees scrubbing floors with Lysol.

Pat and I didn't have much to do, so we took an old World War II jeep and went to patch fences every day. The change in our relationship was quick and almost absolute. He would show up after his seventy-mile drive from Klamath Falls, and I'd still be in bed, nursing a hangover but not so lonesome anymore; I was seeing Patty every couple of nights. He was the man, and I was a boy who needed bossing.

Enormous yellow pines along the far edges of the property stank of sweet pitch as we sat back against them and ate our noontime sandwiches and listened to the 1967 World Series on a portable radio. We drove staples and stretched wire. Contrails crossed the skies. November and winter were coming. Soon it was time to get started gathering the cattle on the Marsh, which were to be sold with the ranch at Warner and trucked out in December. Pat and I hadn't spent time around horses in decades, but Clinton started us easy, on animals we could manage and short days, so we weren't completely crippled. We would ride out over the frozen meadows—the horses farting and grunting, breaking the thin ice as we crossed the sloughs—and after a week or so it was as if I had found my way back to an old dream of how things should be. I loved the rhythms of horseback days and the mist from my breathing as it clouded and blew away on those frozen mornings. Amazingly, I was able to stand at ease while facing myself in the shaving mirror.

This, I thought, might be the place to hide my life. It was a tempting notion, and seemed like a real possibility. Pat and I were talking, stuck together, trying to figure out what to do. Once the ranch was sold we would have the money between us to buy my father's four thousand acres on the Marsh, and we flirted with that old romance, attempting to imagine a future in the ranching business and figure out if we could make a living, if we wouldn't soon be bored, and more important, wondering how long we could stand each other. This, I knew in my heart, would never work. We were going to get just this one chance to make a clean break, and I was spoiled by ambitions I didn't want to talk about; I wanted to be a writer, and had burned some serious bridges. Thank God we had an attack of common sense, took the money, and started the business of fashioning other lives.

The person who got me focused and out of there was Patty. No doubt she was looking for a ticket herself, but we both understood that. It was one of the prime things we shared in our isolation, the belief that we were both imaginative enough to make a getaway. We started off lonely, escaping failures and marriages gone wrong, so it's not surprising that before long we found ourselves irrevocably paired. On good days that fall we would go out to a place called Sagebrush Point, at the edge of a distant field my father owned, overlooking a long sweep of marsh with the Cascades beyond, and we would talk about buying just that piece of property and saving it, and coming back to live there in the faraway future when we were old and secure and the sight of snowcapped mountains would be enough to keep us happy.

Through the early fall we liked to pretend we were a secret, and hadn't committed ourselves to anything beyond talk and play. Then in October, at a branding with neighbors in the corrals by the Losey place where we had run the Mexican steers so many years before, some drinking started and we went public. We ran off together with the afternoon's work unfinished, to Diamond Lake in the high Cascades to the west, where we walked along the shoreline and rhapsodized drunkenly about the elegant reflection of golden leaves shimmering on the quiet lakewater.

We ended up back at the Dinosaur Ranch. Her father was gone, and she was going to cook us a steak dinner. Patty gave me a drink, turned on some classical music, sat me down in a big chair where I could watch, started sharpening a long, deadly-looking knife, and collapsed. Her head struck the countertop, and she fell backward like cloth folding off a hanger, or like someone who'd died. The knife was there on the floor beside her, and blood was beneath her on the floor. I was terrified, and my only thought was that she must have fainted and fallen on the knife. But no, the blood was just soaking out of her Levi's.

I carried her to my pickup and drove the thirty-five miles to the hospital in Klamath Falls at speeds only a drunk is capable of, sure she was dying. They checked her into the emergency room and told me I could leave. No, she was not dying, but she had a history. It was none of my business.

The next day, after scrubbing the blood off the seat in my pickup, I went back to visit. Patty was smiling and sitting up in her hospital bed, bored. She had an ulcerated colon, and one of the ulcers had broken open. "Drinking will kill me," she said, "but not for a long time."

In the way of people who find identity by thinking of themselves as knockabout romantics, we were bonded even if we never were flat honest with each other. In the beginning I think she was in it for the long haul, and she was surely as tough as she needed to be. On a twenty-below blizzarding afternoon she stayed with me while I trailed a dozen cows and their nearly frozen calves in from the swamps. She helped me chop ice with an old double-bitted axe and drove the D-7 Caterpillar, pulling the haysled while I scattered loads of bales across the icy meadows, feeding dry cows. Then, one morning she wouldn't go out. She was pregnant. Driving the icy roads back and forth between Patty's place and the ranch, I listened to country music on my radio, trying to construct an imaginary future in which all of this would be grist for the mill, excited and frightened by the chance that my daydreams of a second life might be coming true, even overwhelmingly true.

I was in Eugene, visiting my mother for Thanksgiving, when we were called to a stockholders' meeting at my grandfather's big house in Klamath Falls, to approve terms for the sale of the ranch. I picked up my sister about four o'clock in the afternoon, and we boozed our way south. Roberta's handsome redheaded husband, Rex, had turned out to be a boy like me, a drinker and runner. They were long since divorced, and she was living in Eugene, raising her kids and seeing people in some bars. Right then we shared a lot of common understandings, and we had a wild high time on that ride. The next morning we were suffering hallucinatory hangovers while everybody sat around avoiding each other's eyes until the business was settled.

The horses of love and familial trust had long since been led to slaughter—all we wanted was a way out of that house. That night Roberta and Pat and I celebrated with a fancy meal, hooting and toasting the gods of good fortune with bottle after bottle of champagne. Nobody had any money in the bank, so we charged it to my father. Roberta gave him the receipt the next day, when he drove her back to Eugene. We'd talked it over and decided she was the only one who could get away with it. She said he laughed and changed the subject. I imagine he was delighted, and maybe thought we would amount to something yet. And anyway, he was starting another life himself.

By mid-December the snow was knee-deep on the flat, and the ponderosas sighed in the winds above my little house near the Williamson River. One vividly cold Sunday morning near Christmas my father came driving in to the Marsh, traveling pretty grandly for that neck of the woods in a new yellow Mercedes, accompanied by his second wife. They parked out front with fog lifting from the tailpipe into the bright, ten-below sunlight. My father came in alone, to ask if I had anything to drink, by which he meant whiskey.

What I had was Jack Daniel's. I poured him a glass, and he asked what I was going to do with myself. I told him I'd be going to Eugene after the first of the year, back to college, to study creative writing, which was not a discipline anybody had ever heard of in our part of the world. I had already spent a weekend in Eugene, with Patty, meeting the people who taught there. My father gave me a serious gray-eyed look, then he almost smiled, and sipped at his tumbler of whiskey, and we began a friendship that lasted until he died.

"I've done work I hated," he said, "all my life, and I sure as hell wouldn't recommend that."

He was reminding me that his life of trying to satisfy his father had in any long sense been a failure. He had suffered five or six heart attacks and a stroke and now was sixty-eight years old and marrying again. He was urging me to get on with my own opportunities.

In Eugene, the summer of 1968, Patty delivered a full-term still-born baby boy. He had strangled on his umbilical cord. "The worst thing," she said, "is the quiet. You can't hear anything but the nurses breathing."

We were married by then, but not long after that she offered to break up in a no-fault sort of way. "Maybe it would be a good idea," she said, "to call it off right now, before we get in any deeper." What she meant was let's not waste any more of our lives, and no doubt she was right, but the idea terrified me. I'd been running to the taverns in my old ways, with my new writer friends. I had indeed found my life, the freedom and chance to turn my obsessions into a profession, and people who thought that was a good idea; but in truth I was as unmoored as I'd ever been, and deeply frightened by the notion of crossing the unexplored territory between me and the Iowa Writers' Workshop. I couldn't imagine going alone.

So I talked Patty into coming along. She saw me through the years of disorientation and foolishness attendant on starting up in the literary life. I was still my own child at heart, selfish as that five-year-old boy who screamed for his mother in the hospital, and as dependent on mothering, running from woman to woman. In the late summer of 1968 we drove east out of Denver, heading to graduate school, and I lost my nerve as the Rocky Mountains sank behind into the expanses of the Nebraska plains. There was nothing out there. This was not my life. I was sick with anomie but there was nothing to turn back toward.

INTERLUDE

A t a very proper New English sort of Thanksgiving dinner, at my grandmother's table, I was seated on a couple of books in a straight-backed chair beside my great-uncle Hank, a dim, lank old alcoholic bachelor with a whiskery beard.

Uncle Hank was munching along in his silent way when he muttered some unintelligible thing and pulled his complete set of false teeth from his mouth, setting them out to dry on the fine white linen tablecloth. Hank's teeth were inextricably tangled with long strings of bright green spinach. They sat there damp and alive, staining the linen cloth, while he went on eating. I began whimpering—what a fool of a child I must have been—and there was a scene. I wish I could remember how it came out. I wish I knew if Uncle Hank was drunk that late afternoon; I wish he was here now.

Uncle Hank used to lie on the lawn in front of the old white-painted ranch house where my grandparents lived when they came to visit their properties in Warner Valley, an aged man flat on his back, watching the birds as they nested. I like to think about Uncle Hank, and what he thought about as he gazed up into the poplars. He was the prime figure of failure in my family: a stranger, the official eccentric, a drunk, a cautionary figure to frighten boys when they were lazy. Hank, it was said, was like a turkey. "He just pecks where he pecks." Which was as much as anybody could make of him. I like to imagine that Uncle Hank was intimate with the habits of birds. I want to tell myself he led a considered life, and knew it was worthwhile to spend his time utterly absorbed in the look of light through the poplar leaves.

I value his indifference to the ambitions which drove my family. He refused to join their scramble to fence the world. I want to believe he was correct, and not just lazy or drunk all the time. I want to think Uncle Hank loved to ride the nesting-ground swamplands in Warner, and thought grid-map plans for reclamation were an abomination, a bad thing in the long run, for us and not just the muskrats and waterbirds. If someone asked, "Who was your model of conduct when you were a child?" I might lie and say Uncle Hank. His is the great-hearted tradition in my family, at least in this version of things.

CHAPTER 9

PARADISE
ALL AROUND

The fall of 1969 I had the good fortune to begin teaching at the University of Montana. Patty and I left Iowa pulling a U-Haul. In South Dakota, at the Missouri River, we crossed back into the West again. The great headwater mountains of Montana, the Beartooths and the Absarokas and the Crazies, when we got in sight of them, loomed like an untouched kingdom. Our first day in Missoula we drove up and down the tree-lined, college-town streets, then I left Patty in the Holiday Inn, did some drinking in a run of taverns, and went unannounced to introduce myself to the main writer in town, the poet Richard Hugo. I marched onto the concrete porch of his little house above the downtown fishing waters where Rattlesnake Creek flows into the Clark Fork River, and rapped a few times. Nothing. I rapped again. Hugo opened his door, a heavy unshaven man in a paint-stained sweatshirt. He studied me like an anthropologist, squinting his eyes. "You're very drunk," he said.

Here, I thought, now you've done it.

"I'll join you," he said.

Maybe this was home.

We wandered out into a field of taverns populated by aged laughing women and pigtailed loggers and motorcycle hippies and cowhands killing time between jobs, and I found friendships which have lasted from then to now. When I first knew him, Dick Hugo lived in a scheme thick with the ghosts of love; he lived in such a way as to make that seem perfectly normal. More than anyone, he helped me convince myself that I wasn't crazy, and that my anxieties were quite usual.

But there wasn't anybody I was supposed to be. A lot of the time I couldn't find myself. I was like a bad detective, searching for significances and afraid to look when I found them, given to getting up in the morning to shower, shave, knock back a little yellow Valium, put on a starched Brooks Brothers shirt, and commence drinking, a childish man who would not let himself think about his children. Escape from the ranch had turned out to be no sort of cure, only a beginning.

The fall of 1973, eager to be someone of consequence and thinking this was the main chance, I accepted a fellowship at Stanford and went off alone. (By this time Patty and I knew our marriage was badly fractured, but we weren't talking about it— maybe some time apart, we thought, maybe that would do the trick.) On my way south, I made a detour to Red Bluff to drive by the house where we lived in 1945, that year of untouchable girls. A long way from anybody I knew, dumb with melancholy, I tried a midafternoon drink, and then another, got in the car and drifted south through the little towns in the Sacramento Valley, sun-struck with alcohol, dreaming of days in the air force, stationed at Travis, when ice cream all around was a major event and things had been so fair with promise in the house where Janet and I had lived with the children when they were small, where my son was born.

The house was gone. There was the asphalt street and a sidewalk running neatly around the block, but the interior of that block was cleared down to bare dirt. No houses, no weeds, bare ground. And a recent job, from the look of it.

Well, you can see this person, half drunk in the afternoon heat, sitting on the front fender of his old Ford while it idles. I was quite familiar with stories in which the loved one comes home after a night out, distant and lying. The solution, I always thought, was to take your pride and walk straight into another dream, which is what that winter in California mostly came to, a lot of pissing in the wind and surviving on the kindness of friends.

Back in Missoula, after that year, Patty and I found our marriage was in ruins. Soon it ended. The energies which brought us together—her willingness to burn her bridges, which always looked like courage, and my determination that I was only up to one thing—drove us apart, and it was never again going to be love above all.

Our man, he was weeping, running the roads, on his own.

Drunk in the morning, fine times with beloved friends . . . this might have been a state of being I learned to value as a child, out on our lawn in the spring light as those great honking flocks of waterbirds passed over on their way north. Except that drunk in the morning was only drunk, and maybe partway deluded, whereas that light and those birds were actual. It was easy to see that a lot of the afternoon sadness in the taverns where I went, mine and everybody else's, had to do with wasted possibilities. Fine capable folks who had discovered nothing to serve but diversion.

For a long time I thought there were no ultimate reasons to discriminate between things which are valuable and those which are not. But in the midst of reinventing myself I began to realize that I had learned some politics on the ranch, by watching the turns of power inside my family. I learned to see my grandfather's fixation on the accumulation of land and money as a bad idea, ultimately and inherently inhumane, an excuse for selfishness, a game mistaken for high purpose. I was driven to believe in damage control, that we must learn to revere and care for the world and one another if we mean to end up with anything of any value at all.

Back in the summer of 1970 Patty and I spent an evening at anchor on Flathead Lake in a spacious old hardwood speedboat. Snowfields on the alpine peaks of the Mission Range were luminous orange in the evening light. We were watching ospreys fall like stones to the black water as they fished for kokanee salmon, which they fed to their young in their huge willow-stick nests on the tiny Oriental-looking Bird Islands.

Except for the yellow-haired stranger wearing mirror-tinted glasses and a gold Rolex (he was rumored to be CIA, back from Asia and looking for a home, and they were thick around town in those days), my companions were local and well-off. They owned timber, a ski area. I said something about DDT, and how it accumulates in the food chain, and what a crime it was that the ospreys were dying out. Contaminated by DDT, they were laying soft-shelled eggs. The stranger took off his dark glasses, and his blue eyes shone. "Fuck birds," he said.

I hung my head and kept quiet but despised this man, who must've dreamt he was born to be merciless. I think of my father sitting on that shell case down by Pelican Lake, shooting ducks for the Elks Club banquet, the long flame in the twilight as he fired, and I love him and can finally acknowledge that I hate the bloodiness.

These were days when a variety of ideals, not to say causes, were available to anybody whose isolation weighed heavily (and, of course, to those who simply believed in them). When the American Indian Movement (AIM) was catching wind in its sails, I wanted to be with them in more than spirit, maybe in some dim way recalling my boyhood friend Vernon Wasson. But the people I met didn't bother to disguise their hostility and disdain, and I was reduced to hustling cases of beer to parties where I wasn't really welcome.

One Saturday night I found myself in a new double-wide trailer on the outskirts of Missoula. I was very drunk, the only white person there. A man was passed out, shirt off, on the coffee table, and three young women were painting his chest with black fingernail polish. It was easy to see the anger of those women as they painted, and easy to imagine that man's fury when he woke up to find his chest all black. I would be the scapegoat at hand. So I went home to my college-professor house with its gleaming hardwood floors and lilacs blooming in the backyard. I tried to put politics out of my head. For a long time it worked. I didn't understand that I had more at stake than my ranch-child sentiments.

Montana has been called a small town with long streets (real long, six hundred miles from the Idaho border to the confluence of the Missouri and the Yellowstone). I walk down Higgins Avenue in Missoula and imagine people who have been dead for a decade, and I miss them. I've spent a morning fishing the streams along the White River syncline in the Bob Marshall Wilderness, and in the afternoon stood looking down on the wilderness elk pastures along the Sun River from the overthrust escarpment of the Chinese Wall. We search for morels under the cottonwoods along sandbars by the Clark Fork River, play golf in the afternoon, go sit on a terrace overlooking the lights of Missoula while we get into the grapefruit juice and Herendura, and sleep at home with the door unlocked. People ask why I live in Montana. I give them answers like that. They're kind of true. It's home.

A friend who lives across the continental divide talks about falling in with "psychic spooks" and driving the prairies for days. "It doesn't do anything for my religious situation," he said, "but it's so beautiful I kind of forget."

Crossing the Rockies at Marias Pass in October, beside the Northern Pacific tracks along the southern edge of Glacier Park, I saw a moose galloping away, swift, huge-headed and spooky like a horse. I was dropping toward East Glacier, where generations of tourists got off Pullman cars to be greeted by Blackfeet Indians wearing authentic beadwork costumes. Beyond were the reservation towns where the Blackfeet actually live. It was spitting snow the next morning in Browning. A knot of men shuffled and blew their noses and told jokes in the parking lot in front of a liquor store, waiting for the doors to open.

In January 1870, the temperature forty below, Major Eugene Baker and his Second U.S. Cavalry attacked a friendly band of Blackfeet-Piegan camped on the Marias River, their lodges full of smallpox victims (it was rumored white traders deliberately gave them the disease with infected blankets). One hundred and seventy-three Indians died. The site of this massacre is an unmarked field by the Marias. The Custer massacre site is a national monument.

James Welch, the Blackfeet writer, tells of driving north into Canada, into the sandhills of the Blackfeet, sacred to his tribe, and finding them covered with dune buggy tracks. "They believed you would go live in the sandhills after you died. It would be like your present life, traveling with your people, and hunting." The Blackfeet, he says, thought they lived someplace close to heaven already. Maybe they thought life was supposed to be the way it already was. Before recreational vehicles.

To the east lay the dryland farming country, strips of crop and fallow ground. The winter wheat is planted in the fall, sprouts, lies dormant through the cold months, and starts growing again in the spring. It is harvested in midsummer, and is the primary dollar crop in Montana. Out on those plains I was in the land of ICBM silos and blizzards, tight white-painted farmsteads, elaborate windbreak tree lines, and (given that a viable wheat farm is worth at least a million) a lot of money. It can be understood as a land of monocultures, both agricultural and spiritual.

Cut Bank, Shelby, Chester, Kremlin, Havre, Chinook, Harlem, Malta, Wolf Point, Poplar: the towns string south of the Canadian border on a route called "the high line," distances from one to another dictated by concerns such as getting crops to the railroad. Their names embody patterns of ethnic settlement and history like a teaching poem about the mix of cultures that might have been: Native American, German-Russian, Dutch, Mediterranean, wolf-hunter.

East of Malta, in the twilight, I saw what looked to be a boy and a girl—one long-haired and the other not, wind-burned faces, skinny ranch kids in their afterschool clothes—carrying damp burlap sacks to cover the late crops against frost in the night. I recall my own childhood with perfect precision, my father's garden and the stinking burlap. I sulked during those hours covering the cucumbers. Darkness came down, bearing the fall brunt of cold. I wondered if those children felt distant from the Great World as I had. Maybe their feelings of insignificance were even more overpowering. I didn't grow up with television and the sight of taillights feathering away into the darkness.

Jordan, Montana (population 485), is frighteningly isolated by any downtown standard. They have a hospital but the nearest doctor is ninety miles away in Miles City. That night in the Hell Creek Bar a handsome woman wanted to dance to the jukebox, but I wouldn't. Nobody else was dancing and I was in the presence of ranchland people: quiet men; Indian women keeping their own company; an overdressed courting couple, trying it out in public; three midcareer cow buyers or bankers or government employees wearing expensive boots, who were talking a lot, too hearty but tolerated; and a lank teenage boy in tennis shoes who was watching his father as his father drank.

There was a time when I belonged in places like that, but I quit the ranch business, and I was sure those people could spot me for a defector. I wanted to stay in my corner and keep quiet like a spy. With a magazine article in mind, I had come with the notion of asking the locals what they thought about a notion known as the Big Open. A dumb idea, asking, since I already knew what they thought: Bad Medicine.

What the Big Open—also known as the Buffalo Commons—amounts to is this: in eastern Montana, adjacent to the Missouri River badlands, there is an enormous expanse (fifteen thousand square miles) of sparsely populated prairie (maybe three thousand inhabitants). Environmentalists argue that this territory constitutes a national treasure, and should be turned into a wildlife preserve, where some three hundred thousand antelopes, deer, elks, and buffalo (and wolves and grizzly bears) could roam as they once did. Biodiversity enshrined is what you'd have. The citizens who live there could make a good living off hunters and the tourist trade. Or, as some call it, the servant business.

To longtime inhabitants of the short-grass plains this is a nightmare. In his 1878 annual report for the United States Geologic Survey, director John Wesley Powell said flatly that the short-grass plains could never be adapted to intensive cropping because of inadequate rainfall and recurrent drought. His report was ignored. By 1910 James Hill had built his Great Northern Railroad across northern Montana—thus creating the high line—and he was trying to sell tickets, claiming 320 acres would support a homestead farm. In a mass migration settlers came to the plains bearing possessions; they built shacks and they tried to farm; most of them failed, and most of them left, having wasted years in dirt-eating poverty. Most citizens of Jordan are descendants of the survivors, and now they find social scientists talking about turning their homeland into a preserve for wild beasts. They are angry and humiliated, justifiably.

They think environmentalists value the goddamned buffalo more than they value the sacrifices of their people. I imagined telling people in Jordan I thought the Buffalo Commons held at least the seed of a necessary idea. It is our duty to preserve huge tracts of land in something resembling its native condition. The biological interactions necessary to ensure the continuities of life are astonishingly complex, and cannot take place in islands of semiwilderness like the national parks. A hundred and fifty years ago some sixty million buffalo roamed the North American prairies. The last wild ones were shot south of Jordan in 1886, by William Hornaday, a taxidermist, for display in the Smithsonian. He went back to Washington, D.C., with twenty-four hides, sixteen skeletons, and fifty-one skulls—the nineteenth-century way of preserving the last wild buffalo. I imagined telling the people in Jordan, "We're taking your land, we're kicking you out. We're sorry, but our purposes are larger than yours."

I imagined telling them we needed to replant the world and make it holy again. I imagined explaining the mental health of our species, and how good it is for our sanity to witness nature at its most multitudinous—flocks of waterbirds beyond numbering and sixty million buffalo and on to life everlasting; in our imaginations such encounters function as a sight of possibility. Maybe I could tell them we continue to inhabit an age of sacred beasts, even as we destroy them. I could have said destroying them is a way of destroying ourselves.

No doubt I would have been dismissed as another nitwit missionary, come to take everything they had suffered for. The people in Jordan have good reason to go xenophobic, not so much fearing strangers as despising them. In a place like the Hell Creek Bar in Jordan, Montana, talking about the Big Open would probably be a good way to get your ass kicked.

But those good people might have told me paradise is all around. They might have told me to take a walk into the world, which I did. The next morning I saw a broom-tailed fox on the outskirts of Jordan. A great blue heron flew under the highway bridge and came out on the other side.

> . . . and a last love, which, being last, will be like looking up and seeing the parachute dissolving in a shower of gold.
>
> —GALWAY KINNELL,
> "The Road Between Here and There"

Annick Smith has been the luck of my later life, a widow of Jewish and Hungarian blood, mother of four grown boys, and willing to stay humane no matter how disconcerted she might be in her heart, or pissed off at the wayward fragility of things. She is a good deal less flighty than I am when anything like the ultimate chips are falling. While their children watched, she spent half an hour crouched and trying to force breath back into her husband's mouth after he had fallen into death on their kitchen floor. Annick has been tempered by circumstance in ways that I have not. But don't worry, her life seems to say, you'll get your chance, soon enough.

So Annick had little patience with me in the spring of 1979 when I found out my daughter was going to be wed in Ashland, Oregon, where Janet had settled her life. "You're going," she said, "of course." I hadn't seen my children or Janet in more than ten years, or even talked to them on the telephone. Or written. Now there was a chance to begin some healing, at least with my children, a prospect that terrified me. I persuaded Annick to come with me, and hold my aging hand.

The night before the ceremony I sat in a restaurant with Annick and my brother, Pat, a little drunk, panicked, and ready to cut and run. They laughed at me, at the fearfulness of a stubborn dimwitted child. Janet must have worried that I would show up in some chemical state, which would have confirmed her worst apprehensions. But in the light of the next morning I was calm and dull, walking through a performance. We had loved and depended on one another, and now we were strangers, and I was determined to be untouchable.

But I couldn't be. Karen, the bride, my daughter, with her beauty and power, seemed determined this was to be another beginning, on her terms. Janet and I weren't calling the shots anymore. I bit my lip after Karen turned to me and recognized me, and came to me, so far as I could tell, without resentment or embarrassment. As she was married, up there with her new husband and the lilies around her, I thought this might be a new world. Afterward a bartender ignited a series of drinks and my son took to knocking them back, blue flames at his mouth. Brad grinned and challenged me to try one. I turned him down, but for a quick fearful moment we had looked each other in the eye. Janet had raised them to be more courageous than I was.

On the way home Annick and I toured the desert country of southeastern Oregon, a ritual of courting that made sense to me. I felt blessed when she discovered flowers in the rimrocks above Sage Hen Springs. As a boy on those deserts I had never noticed them. She seemed comfortable in the silence ringing over the distances. "Pretty abstract," I said, and she understood me to mean everything I had learned to see as real.

We stood at ten thousand feet in the air of daybreak over the ridgetop of Steens Mountain, the great rockfall to the alkaline playa of the Alvord Desert just at our backs. We could see the Pine Forest Mountains of Nevada and Bidwell Mountain in California. The snowy ghost of Mount Adams, in the state of Washington, hung dim against the horizon like a phantom sail.

We could smell the wash of ozone from a run of lightning storms the night before, an odor like something to taste. I felt myself vividly alive, maybe because we were gazing onto the country I always see in my mind when I start to tell myself about my life: Catlow Valley, where homesteaders lured west by railroad promotions built their cabins and cleared their land and planted rye and failed in such absolute ways in the 1920s; and East Road Gulch in the Beatty Buttes, where we made a sport of killing rattlesnakes one morning when I was a boy; and the Hart Mountain escarpment, which I see as I saw it from the fields we were harvesting in early September, luminous in the evening light of the 1960s.

My people drained the swamps and farmed them, and built roads and fences across the enormous sweep of that country as if they were inscribing their names onto the land. This is ours, they said, we own it. But they didn't, not in any significant way. Despite the paved roads and the irrigation agriculture in the valleys and the decades of overgrazing and the long runs of drift fence on the deserts, most of that country looks naturally intact from far away, and sometimes from close up in the flowering enclaves.

We drove down from sunrise on Steens Mountain, crossing gravel roads on the northern edges of Catlow Valley to the break over Hart Mountain into North Warner, where we could look down on lakes brimming with spring runoff, shimmering in the morning breezes, edged with green and populated by rafts of white pelicans and snow geese. We stood facing such beauty as if given something from a dream about what the world could be, if we let it, alive and significant without us.

No doubt I was to some slight degree flirting with my old insanities, wetting my finger and touching the hot stovetop another time, saying "See, it can't happen anymore." In Guano Valley we turned onto a rough Bureau of Land Management road, heading toward Lone Grave Butte and beyond, to a place we called Rock Springs when I was a boy, on the northern edges of the Beatty Buttes. Up behind the cabin at Rock Springs is a cliff maybe a hundred feet high. I wanted to sit there looking out at the world one more time, something I hadn't done since I was fourteen, and found I could recall each handhold in the rock, but only as I saw it or reached to touch it. It was as if I was the lost piece falling into a puzzle.

Toward sunset we were making our way across northern Nevada, through the Sheldon Antelope Refuge, and stunned by what seemed an infinity of antelope in little bands of two or three or eight or fifteen grazing the grassy edges of an alkaline playa. They paid us none of their sweet attention, but went on grazing in intricate syncopation, leaving us to witness a sight from the enormous isolations of the past, a song we've always known and make our meanings from.

Our old pilgrims believed stories in which the West was a promise, a place where decent people could escape the wreckage of failed lives and start over. Come along, the dream whispers, and you can have another chance. We still listen to promises in the wind. This time, we think, we'll get it right.

My grandfather's first property, the River Ranch at Summer Lake, where I ran my hay baler the summer of 1967 while my marriage was dissolving, is now a wildlife refuge belonging to the Oregon State Fish and Game Commission. The ranch at Warner has been sold and resold, and there's a distinct possibility it will eventually be part of a great sweep of territory, millions of acres in a mosaic of federal, state, and privately held properties across those landlocked valleys and deserts and mountains, all dedicated to biodiversity, a scheme quite like the Buffalo Commons in the working out. If so the redwood weirs my father built, the drainage canals and pumps, may be torn out, and the swamps may refill with spring runoff, to evolve back into tulebeds, and the waterbirds may come back in flocks beyond numbering. Or maybe not. Maybe those flocks don't exist anymore.

Our years of labor would have come to nothing, and that would be fine with me. I have a stake in the outcome: I want to ensure that my children's grandchildren can walk out into spring mornings which reek of life like the ones I knew.

We are animals evolved to live in the interpenetrating energies of all the life there is, so far as we know, which coats the rock of earth like moss. We cannot live, I think, without connection both psychic and physical, and we begin to die of pointlessness when we are isolated, even if some of us can hang on for a long while connected to nothing beyond our imaginations.

We must define a story which encourages us to make use of the place where we live without killing it, and we must understand that the living world cannot be replicated. There will never be another setup like the one in which we have thrived. Ruin it and we will have lost ourselves, and that *is* craziness.

I want the animals lying down with one another, and fecundity, one seduction and another until we are all satisfied with our lives, children playing on sandy beaches by a stream, in the warm shade of the willows, the flash of salmon in the pools. Children of your own as only you can see them. It's just a moment I imagine, nothing real about it. But I wonder why. How do we understand our kingdom?

I want to think that all creatures, even us, are in love with the makeup of their actualities like bats at the throat of some desert flower while no one is watching, spreading pollen in ways the flower would love if flowers did such things. And maybe they do.

My father told of his father transporting all his family in horse-drawn wagons on ill-made trails across the Cascades from the alkaline country around Silver Lake, Oregon, to spend three weeks in the fall, canning fruit and vegetables just south of Corvallis. He told of the eagerness with which his family looked forward to the difficulties of that journey.

When it came his turn, my father escaped the desert and went to live in Brookings, on the Oregon coast, with his second wife. People who grow up on deserts seem driven to the sea, which they imagine as the source of possibility. They kept track of how many salmon they took over the transom of their boat each season, mostly to be canned and given away, as if the fishing was another version of gin rummy. She died of leukemia, and he got too unsteady to go on the ocean alone, so he sat through the rainy days smoking his pipe, and seemed more at peace than anybody. A lot of the time he didn't even bother looking toward the long horizon over the Pacific.

Though my father died in the spring of 1990, he's still alive in my imagination. I wouldn't be surprised to turn and see him at the rail in some Montana tavern, eyeing me with his old irony, tapping his Shriner's money clip on the bar while the tattooed bartender pours his drink, which was scotch and milk at the end, for his angina.

The drive wore him out the last time he came to Montana. He was eighty-seven, going on nine heart attacks. "The next one," he said, "and I'm out of lives, like a house cat." He grinned, and I openly admired his style. We'd drive into another hummingbird day in the Bitterroot Valley, which can be thought of as a kind of out-West Shangri-La, a happy kingdom surrounded by wilderness mountains. We stopped at a bridge over the river and watched yellow rafts coming at us, fishermen in the morning, fly lines flashing in the sun. "They'll never see it," my father said.

Partly, I understood, he was talking about the way the world was disappearing, the luck of his life and what had come of it, and the Bitterroot Valley as evidence of loss. Black cattle grazed belly-deep in meadows by the river. Rain-Bird sprinklers were throwing rainbows over the alfalfa benchlands. Much of that valley looks like a dream of heaven out of some Jeffersonian Book of Days but the roadsides are built up with shops and parlors—beauty, plumbing, welding, fencing, chain saw, ranchette realtor, taxidermy. "They got it turned into a goddamned trailer park," he said. My father was talking about things I would never see, a past that looked more valuable than any foreseeable future. He was talking about regret, and telling himself he was ready to die. Or maybe he was done telling himself. Maybe he was telling me.

My friends have begun dying, people of my generation, and I do not have anything like a set of consolations for my own fragility. I am irreligious as a stone and no more profound or coherent in my thinking about such things than I was at age eleven. Let it go, I figured then and still think now. There's plenty of time, you'll think of something.

No such luck. It is time we lay hands on a sustaining mythology. I examine my beliefs, if that's what they are, and they feel more like dreams. I have come to believe what I believed as a child: these things are all we have, and they resonate with all the significance there is ever going to be.

After Oscar died, nobody wept, at least not in sight of anyone else. My mother looked at me in her most direct way, from her bed in her nursing home in Salem. "He was the only man," she said, "that I ever wanted to marry." I wonder what they saw in their most private vision of the right life, what they saw in each other and everything else.

Janet is married and lives in Corvallis. Patty lives in San Diego. My brother, Pat, is a good man in Klamath Falls, where we went to high school just those four decades ago. My sister, Roberta, is married to a construction steelworker. They plan to retire to a little place in the timber country south of Bend. Karen lives in Portland with her husband and four boys. Brad lives on Vashon Island, a short boat ride from Seattle, with his wife.

My mother wanted a life of consequence and feels she missed it. My father wanted to live out his life surrounded by friends and family, and fields of his own designing. The last time I saw him he was a fragile old man asleep in a chair, and didn't know me when he woke. "Bill's coming," he said, and then he looked at me and laughed in his old way. "Who the hell did I think you were?" he said, and we both laughed. "I'm getting a little stronger," he said. "A couple of weeks and I'm going to be back on the streets." He grinned again, and I couldn't tell if he thought the notion was funny or not. A few days later he drifted into a coma. We got word he would soon be gone, and he was. His ashes were scattered over the deserts east of Warner, in country where he'd gone with his friends to hunt mule deer and drink scotch whiskey and play poker in the light of a kerosene lantern, and tell stories on one another, which in his book was the real world.

In extreme old age my mother understands, as my father did, that knowing the story of your people in gossipy detail means you're nearer to placing yourself in relationship to what is called the blood of things. I tell my own stories, and I move a little closer toward feeling at home in the incessant world, but I can't imagine where I would want my ashes scattered, not yet.

If we want to be happy at all, I think, we have to acknowledge that the circumstances which encourage us in our love of this existence are essential. We are part of what is sacred. That is our main defense against craziness, our solace, the source of our best politics, and our only chance at paradise.

A NOTE ON THE TYPE

The text of this book was set in Weiss, a type face designed in Germany by Emil Rudolf Weiss (1875–1942). The design of the roman was completed in 1928 and that of the italic in 1931. Both are well balanced and even in color, and both reflect the subtle skill of a fine calligrapher.

Composed by Creative Graphics,
Allentown, Pennsylvania

Printed and bound by
Fairfield Graphics,
Fairfield, Pennsylvania

Designed by Cassandra J. Pappas